For my children, Natalie, Hayley and Tom.

The Murder that Defeated Whitechapel's Sherlock Holmes

The Murder that Defeated Whitechapel's Sherlock Holmes

At Mrs Ridgley's Corner

Paul Stickler

PEN & SWORD HISTORY

First published in Great Britain in 2017 by
PEN AND SWORD HISTORY
an imprint of
Pen and Sword Books Ltd
47 Church Street
Barnsley
South Yorkshire S70 2AS

ISBN 978 1 52673 385 6

Printed and bound by CPI Group (UK) Ltd, Croydon, CR0 4YY

Typeset in Times New Roman by
Aura Technology and Software Services, India

Pen & Sword Books Ltd incorporates the imprints of Pen & Sword
Archaeology, Atlas, Aviation, Battleground, Discovery,
Family History, History, Maritime, Military, Naval, Politics, Railways,
Select, Social History, Transport, True Crime, Claymore Press,
Frontline Books, Leo Cooper, Praetorian Press, Remember When,
Seaforth Publishing and Wharncliffe.

For a complete list of Pen and Sword titles please contact
Pen and Sword Books Limited
47 Church Street, Barnsley, South Yorkshire, S70 2AS, England
E-mail: enquiries@pen-and-sword.co.uk
Website: www.pen-and-sword.co.uk

Contents

Acknowledgements

Writing and researching for this book has been an immensely enjoyable journey and there a few people I would like to thank. First of all to the body of professional archivists who always seem to know where to find helpful information, particularly Michael Lynch, archivist at Kerry Library, Tralee, who was tremendously helpful in locating documents about Listowel and John Healy's family and Stefan Dickers at the Bishopsgate Institute in London who pointed me in the right direction of valuable information regarding Fred Wensley. Equal thanks go to Nick Connell at the Hertfordshire Archives and Local Studies, Hertfordshire County Council and to the Hertfordshire Constabulary Historical Society for the assistance they provided. I owe a deal of gratitude to Derek Stevens, Curator and Secretary of the Hampshire Constabulary History Society who stumbled across original and exciting material and brought it to my attention and to Dr Clifford Williams of the same Society for pointing me in the right direction. I extend similar thanks to Marc Thompson for his invaluable help in researching military records. For reading my manuscript and providing me with extremely helpful feedback, I would like to thank Mark Jones, Colin Smith, Natalia Sabadas and Andy Williams. Finally, for providing encouragement and instilling in me a genuine belief that this project could be done I want to extend a special thank you to Dan Clacher, Moira Anderson and again, Natalia Sabadas. Without each of you, I may well have given up.

Paul Stickler,
September 2017

Introduction

Murder narratives are relatively commonplace and occupy a prominent position in the public imagination. The enduring fascination with people's behaviour seems never-ending, particularly when it involves the ultimate act of violence and the quest to find out who was responsible. Many cases will remain in the memories of people for considerable time such has been the amount of attention that has been paid to quite extraodinary events in the past.

Every now and again, though, an unwritten story, hidden away in dusty archives, rises to the surface which has received no attention, no analysis and involving someone who has been long forgotten. *At Mrs Ridgley's Corner* is such a case, a victim buried in an unmarked grave, her plight unknown and consigned to history. Her story needs to be told for it has an important contribution to make to understand a piece of history, to throw light on rural policing immediately after the First World War and, importantly, ensure she is not forgotten.

I have chosen to adopt a different approach to the conventional method of analysis, preferring instead to examine the detail through the eyes and emotions of the characters involved, as if the reader was there listening to their thoughts, and without a narrative which has the benefit of knowing what is yet to come. Such an approach gives the reader a greater understanding of not only what happened, but why. The decisions taken by the police, by neighbours and other key actors are seen through an untainted lens, and in the order it happened.

There are no assumptions made about any of the characters involved, no unnecessary dramatisation, but rather it draws on the original material, documents and photographs, which exposes suffcent drama in itself.

It is, ultimately, an account which would, I hope, address the frustrations of those who were involved and if it was of course possible, allow the victim lying in her grave, to rest a little more in peace.

'Where a person of sound memory and discretion – unlawfully killeth – any reasonable creature in being – and under the King's Peace – with malice aforethought – either express or implied – he shall be guilty of murder.' (Edward Coke 1552-1634)

'I, _____, do swear that I will well and truly serve our Lord The King in the office of Constable for the County of Hertfordshire, without favour or affection, malice or ill-will: and that I will to the best of my power cause the peace to be kept and preserved, and prevent all offences against the persons and properties of His Majesty's subjects: and that while I continue to hold the said office I will to the best of my skill and knowledge discharge all the duties thereof faithfully according to law. So help me God.' (Police Oath of Office)

Chapter 1

Death on the Corner

Hertfordshire, Saturday, 25 January 1919

Unusually, the front door was open. A dim light shone from inside. People who passed the grocer's shop on the corner of Garden Row and Nightingale Road in the Hertfordshire town of Hitchin thought it odd but ignored it. Saturday, 25 January was a bitterly cold night, snow thick on the ground, sleet blown into the faces of the few who braved the weather. It wasn't the night to hang around; a night to be at home in front of the fire. Everyone knew that at nine o'clock Mrs Ridgley routinely closed her shop, locked the front door and extinguished the paraffin lamp in her converted front room, but perhaps she was busy dealing with a customer. Ten minutes later, the front door was closed, its blind still up and the lamp still emitted its faint glow. Unusual, but those who saw it were more concerned about getting home.[1]

The following morning, Sunday, Gertrude Day edged carefully along Garden Row having twice already slipped up on the fresh snow that had fallen overnight. As she approached the junction, taking her alongside the rear of Mrs Ridgley's shop, she saw the back door open and subconsciously expected to see the 54-year-old woman either emerge or to see her somewhere in the back garden, but she saw only the small, cluttered yard, though barely visible through the six feet of untidy hedgerow.[2] Sheets of wood leant against the back wall and a couple of wooden boxes were piled on top of one another. She saw the piece of loose fence trellis which the grocer used at the entrance to her back door to keep her Irish terrier dog in the garden in the summer, a water butt hard against the rear scullery wall and a drainpipe awkwardly placed above it to catch the water from the gutter. Now, its chaotic appearance was masked by the heavy snow and the icicles hanging dramatically from the guttering. Other than noticing that the back gate to the garden appeared to be firmly closed, she thought no more and concentrated on maintaining her footing on the slippery surface. As she turned the corner and passed the front door of the shop, nothing caught her attention. It was, after all, a Sunday and everything was closed.

At half past eight the following morning, she returned. She needed matches and firewood, and as she approached the front door, she saw schoolchildren giggling, trying to peer through the window. The door was closed and the blind drawn down on the inside. Strange, she thought, since Mrs Ridgley always opened up at eight o'clock and she was sure that the weather wouldn't have put her off from trading as normal. She tried opening the door but it was locked. She banged again and called out. She had known the shopkeeper for nine years, since she had moved to Hitchin, and had got to know her fairly well, particularly since she had become widowed two years earlier. There was no response and so she banged the door again.

There was still no reply, so she made her way back to St Saviour's Working Men's Club some eighty yards away where she worked as a caretaker and returned an hour later.[3] With still no answer to her repeated banging, and the blind still drawn on the inside, she walked into Garden Row, where she could see the back of the house. Nothing appeared to have changed, and alarmingly, the back door was still open. There was no sign of Mrs Ridgley and no sign of her dog, which never left her side. Something was wrong. She was deciding what to do next when a neighbour, James Knight, appeared who told her that he had also tried to enter the shop but found the door locked. Now beginning to panic a little, she explained what she had done and they agreed to go to the police station in the centre of town. They reported their concerns to the sergeant behind the desk, and Police Constable Alfred Kirby, an officer with nearly six years' service, was instructed to accompany the couple back to the shop to investigate further. They arrived at twenty past ten.[4]

Constable Kirby went through the same routine of banging and shouting. He went round to the side of the house and saw that the gate to the back garden was padlocked from the inside. He had been here before; Mrs Ridgley had been involved in a house fire the previous May and he and PC 187 Josiah Selby had helped to rescue her. He reflected on this for a while, remembering the details. The shopkeeper had needed to be carried from the premises suffering from suffocation and had been taken to hospital, and once he had managed to examine the house he found that there had been a small fire in the rear living room. On the table, there had been a bottle of gin, and having spoken to her later it appeared as though she had become ill in her kitchen, collapsed and was completely unaware of the fire that had developed, probably caused by a paraffin lamp she had fallen on. Had she done the same thing again, he wondered, as he stood staring at the back door? He also recalled that she had a dog, and he whistled in an attempt to arouse the animal, but there was no response.

Other neighbours were beginning to gather at the shop door, shaking its handle and shouting through the letterbox. Two men approached Kirby to see if they could help. The constable announced he was going into the house and asked them both to accompany him.[5]

As Kirby approached the back door, he made a mental note that it was three-quarters open and the blind on the inside of the living room was fully down. This was where the fire had been the previous year. At the door, he shouted once again to get the attention of the shopkeeper but got the same result. He stepped into the house, feeling no discernible increase in air temperature, and moved slowly forward, his eyes scanning around the small kitchen. Turning right into the scullery, or at least a room which was seemingly used more as some sort of storage area, he continued to peer into the house, his eyes squinting as they adjusted to the poor light. Just inside the door, crates of sugar neatly piled on top of one another rested alongside a large pile of new broom heads. Next to them, a cloth protected something piled halfway up the wall, masking the worn and heavily tarnished floral wallpaper. On the opposite side, he could see a flour barrel with a set of scales sitting on the top, a pestle resting in its cradle. Although filled with shop provisions, the room still had the appearance of being tidy – busy, but organised. The floor, though, was empty, an obvious pathway running through to the hallway which led to the front of the house and the room which had been converted to a shop.

With the two men still behind him, Kirby slowly crossed the scullery floor heading for the hallway. His eyes adjusted to the darkness and could see his breath in the air silhouetted against the faint light emanating from the opened back door. He moved further into the house, the light gradually diminishing. Suddenly, he stopped. His eyes had acclimatised and he could see the clear outline of someone lying on the floor, the head resting against the bottom of the stairs, the torso across the width of the hallway, the lower half of the body disappearing into the entrance to the living room. With no torchlight to assist him, he turned back to the scullery to retrieve a candlestick he had seen, lit it, and went back. With more light, all three men could now see the body of a fully clothed woman face down on the floor, her arms resting underneath her chest and what appeared to be a cloth wrapped around her neck. Peering into the doorway to the right, Kirby could see the woman's legs outstretched but with her heels facing upwards and her toes pointing towards the floor. The neighbour who had followed the constable in stepped carefully over the body, went to the rear of the living room and opened the heavy set of curtains which were hanging untidily over the rear window. He raised the blind behind them and daylight spread instantly across the prostrate body.

The other man who had accompanied Kirby into the house immediately remarked, 'She's been done in,'[6] and pointed to her head, which was saturated in blood and resting on top of a piece of sacking, probably a doormat, itself heavily bloodstained. Even though the body was face down, the man, who had known Mrs Ridgley for seven years, instantly recognised her, and he confirmed her identity to the constable.

Elizabeth Ridgley had run the corner shop by herself in recent years and many had commented that she was rather a serious woman who rarely smiled and was very focused on making money from her business. She had few friends, no children from her marriage and probably her only real companion in life was her Irish terrier dog. A lonely woman, who now lay dead in the passageway of her house.

Kirby slowly surveyed the hallway. He immediately noticed an iron weight resting on the floor two feet from the woman's head. His mind was racing; if she had been murdered, was this the weapon which had been used to attack her? He crouched down and picked it up, not really knowing what he was looking for, though he could clearly see that it was covered in blood and had short, gingers hairs stuck to the bottom of it. He put it back down again, making sure he returned it to the exact same place. He touched the side of Ridgley's face and neck and quickly realised the body was cold. He stood up, examining the passageway in more detail, still trying to understand what he was looking at. Halfway between the body and the weight, an empty cigar box caught his attention. Looking back towards the scullery, he stared at the scales he had seen just a few minutes earlier. He now knew where the weight had come from.

A makeshift structure of wooden planks, measuring about three feet square, and which he recognised as a dog-gate used by Ridgley to keep her pet from going into the shop during opening hours, rested against the stairs. He turned towards the front of the house and suddenly jolted. He was staring at the body of a motionless dog lying on its left side further along the

4

hallway and facing the front door. He instantly recognised it as the grocer's Irish terrier and saw a large gathering of foam next to its mouth and three motions where it had clearly evacuated its bowels; one immediately next to its rear end, another in the passageway and the third in the living room. The dog lay about three feet away from its owner. Kirby, now realising what he was dealing with, instructed one of the men who had come into the house with him to go to the police station, raise the alarm and fetch a doctor. With two dead bodies to deal with, it was going to be a busy day, and more cold and snow was on its way.

Chapter 2

Outbreak of War

Ireland, 1910

John Healy was sitting in the prisoner's dock inside the quarter sessions court building in Tralee, County Kerry. He had been at the magistrates' court three years ago, when he was fined for being drunk, but this was different. Yet he was unconcerned and briefly allowed himself a glance at the two prisoners in the dock with him. His brother Thomas and their friend John Browne looked smart in their suits. They always did when they dressed up, quite different from their farm labourers' trousers and shirts which they usually wore when herding cows in their field at Listowel. It was cold inside the building. The winter of 1910 was bitter but they were sitting patiently listening to the proceedings droning on in front of them. Their solicitor was doing a good job and had already shown the alleged victim in the case to be someone who couldn't really remember anything. Unlawfully and feloniously assaulting Patrick Keogh was the charge, but in cross-examination he had failed to identify the three prisoners in the dock. Not surprisingly perhaps. He had been kicked half to death and had his teeth knocked out as he had walked through Listowel town centre. He remembered being confronted by three men who had asked him for a light for a cigarette, but after that everything had been a blur. He vaguely recalled being pushed up against an archway, into a passageway, and then took several blows to the head and legs before collapsing unconscious. He had been laid up for two weeks, unable to work, and whoever had done this had stolen the fourteen shillings he had in his pocket. He was permanently dizzy and was scared to go out of his house now. The defendants listened dispassionately.

The prosecution then called their other witnesses. Publicans in the small market town spoke of the three men drinking all afternoon in their pubs, and a barmaid, Mary Enright, working in Stack's public house saw them walk past heading towards the archway where Keogh had been attacked. They disappeared from view, and very shortly afterwards she went out the back of the pub to close a gate and saw the victim lying unconscious on the ground. She looked up and saw the same three men running away. She had called for them to stop but they'd kept going.

Once again, the solicitor rose to his feet and told the judge that he considered the case too weak, with only one witness who could say that she saw the defendants in the area at the time. This didn't prove the case, nor did it mean that just because his clients were drinking nearby that they could reasonably be held to be responsible. He asked the judge to direct the jury to find the prisoners not guilty on the grounds of insufficient evidence. The judge, Stephen Woulfe-Flanagan considered the application and directed the jury to find the prisoners 'not guilty'. The Healy brothers and their friend walked free from court.

Mons, Belgium, 23 August 1914

Healy stared down at the face looking back at him. If it could talk it would be begging for help, but the bottom half of the jaw was missing and the man was bleeding badly from his stomach. His eyes were doing the talking. Healy thought about leaving him and moving on to the next soldier lying a few feet away, but somehow his conscience got the better of him and he pulled out some bandages from his bag and tried to stem the flow of blood.

He reacted instinctively to the occasional bombardment of German shells landing nearby, wondering when his turn would come but focussed on getting the Royal Irish infantryman on a stretcher and hauled back to the advanced dressing station. Not that it would be easy. The Royal Army Medical Corps had been caught by surprise as much as every other British soldier who was dug into trenches on the outskirts of Mons. They hadn't prepared for this. Only minor skirmishes were expected they'd been told as they'd marched from Le Havre to the Belgian border, often covering fifteen miles in a day, but all of a sudden, the merciless and ruthless reality of war had hit them full on. Only the night before they'd established a hospital a few miles away in Dour but they'd suddenly been sent forward to deal with Allied soldiers who had been cut down by German lancers and machine-gun fire as the two enemies met for the first time at the Mons-Condé canal. Stretcher bearers were not normally deployed during battle; their role began once firing had finished. But there seemed no obvious end. A break in the shelling was followed by the order for them to go forward, but then the firing started again and only a few days after the first shots had been fired, the allies were in retreat.

Another soldier helped Healy clumsily bundle the injured man onto a stretcher and he moved on to the next casualty. He was already dead, half his left leg missing. A severed arm rested a few feet away, its owner nowhere to be seen. A shell landed thirty feet away and the blast knocked him over, but he stood up and walked towards a soldier waving and shouting at him. The side of his face was ripped open by shrapnel, but he was more in shock than anything else. Healy pulled him up, and with the injured man's arm slung around his shoulder, he walked him back towards the trenches.

This was all a far cry from what he had expected when he had casually joined the Royal Munster Fusiliers back in County Kerry in 1903. Being a farm labourer was not what he had wanted, and the army offered him a regular wage. He had even performed well in his army exams, been promoted to lance corporal and been posted out to Gibraltar for eighteen months, but when he left three years later as a reservist, he hadn't expected a full-scale war to break out. No one had. When he wasn't being arrested by the police for being drunk or for things he hadn't done, he had transferred as a reservist to the Medical Corps but when Britain declared war on Germany he was swiftly recruited in to the regular army and put onto the *Archimedes* supply ship in Dublin, destination France. Over by Christmas, they said, and on the way across the troops had all sung 'God save the King'. They'd marched up from the French coast to rapturous applause from French villagers who had decorated their houses in Union Jacks; this was all going to be another soft touch, like Gibraltar. That was on 16 August 1914, and now here he was, a week later, facing the full force of the Battle of Mons as part of 13th Field Ambulance. The war was turning into a barbaric exchange of mutilating explosives between invisible enemies.

Healy was never quite sure why Ireland was fighting in the first place. The British government had agreed to Irish Home Rule and it was only a matter of time, once the short war in France was over, that Ireland would be a separate country. There was already strong anti-British sentiment in the country so fighting alongside them didn't make a lot of sense to him. Not that he was the only Irishman here; there were hundreds, including the Royal Irish Regiment. But, as he now recovered injured soldiers, he didn't have much time to reflect on that, and in a rather accepting mood he moved among the dead and injured. The battle had started early that morning, with the British trying to defend a seemingly indefensible canal system, and as the day progressed there was an endless onslaught of German artillery fire followed by swathes of German soldiers flocking towards them, themselves being slaughtered by British snipers. The Germans retreated, reformed, and, apparently under threat of being shot by their own officers for cowardice, they ran forward again. Hundreds of soldiers, British and German, were being cut down each time, and the field ambulance teams ran along behind picking up the pieces. At one point, Healy couldn't believe his eyes when, instead of the German Army rushing forward, he saw a group of frightened schoolchildren running towards him. They were panicking. The whole town was panicking. Their routine had been suddenly shattered and thousands of men were being blown apart and shot. German spotter planes dropped smoke bombs designed to both confuse the enemy and give a target for German artillery fire, exploding shells indiscriminately, blasting shrapnel into faces, and the regiments of the British army had been transformed from one of high spirits and jingoism to one in complete shock and devastation in the space of a few hours. As the German bugle sounded at the end of the day for a ceasefire, there were 5,000 German casualties and 1,600 British soldiers dead, wounded or missing. The Royal Irish Regiment had lost 300 men.

1916

The euphoria and glory of being at war quickly disappeared, and Healy became used to seeing death and the agonies of wounded soldiers. He would always remember 11 May 1915, when he was attending a wounded soldier who had been hit by exploding shrapnel and he was hit in the hand by one of the hundreds of German bullets that were coming his way. His short trip home for rehabilitation came as a welcome respite, and though he was sent back out to the Mediterranean shortly afterwards, it wasn't long before the day came when he could leave the army. The war was still raging, but in 1916, having finished his thirteen-year commitment, he headed back to Listowel. For the past two years he had been exposed to the extremes of violence, had earned the right to wear the 1914 Star, the British War Medal and the Victory Medal and being a farm labourer again, now had a certain attraction.

Chapter 3

Blood Everywhere

Hertfordshire, Monday, 27 January 1919

Heavy snow was now falling on the streets, the temperature had dropped further, but inside 125 Nightingale Road, Constable Kirby wasn't going to sit and do nothing while he waited for his colleagues and the doctor to arrive. This looked very much like a murder to him, he thought, as he stared at the two motionless bodies in the passageway. He had been waiting for an opportunity like this to show that he was more able than merely patrolling the streets of Hitchin. Six years he had been in the Hertfordshire Constabulary and now something had turned up for him to get his teeth into.

Even as a constable, Kirby knew that the old-style beat system, which had been around since police were installed on the rural streets of Britain in the 1830s, was out of date and useless. Every day, he and his colleagues were made to stand to attention in the police station while the sergeant briefed them on break-ins and drunkenness in the town, many constables not even paying attention. Their truncheon and pocketbooks checked, they were then made to march in single-file around the town dropping officers at their appointed beats, the same place and time every day. They were then required to walk at a fixed pace and to be at the next point at an agreed time to meet the sergeant who would often just send them off on the next part of their beat with no further useful information to give. They were not even allowed to 'stand and gossip' with the residents on their beats for fear of becoming too close and susceptible to bribes. For anyone who wanted to commit crime, they merely had to wait for the constable to pass his point at the appointed time and he knew they had at least half an hour before another policeman would be in the area. For years he had slogged around like this but now he had a real crime to get excited about.

Inside the shop, he continued in his hunt for clues and looked again at the two items lying next to the murdered woman; the cigar box and the weight. The box was bloodstained, and had no lid, but there were two unused red-top Vesta matches lying inside. A number of used matches lay on the floor close to the body. Did this tell him that whatever happened was carried out at night? It gets dark so early this time of year, he thought, as he continued to piece together what he was looking at. The weight, about three feet away from Ridgley's head, was oblong in shape, standing upright. The inscription on the top told him it weighed four pounds (just under 2kg) and he sucked back through his teeth as he imagined the heavy object cracking down on the woman's skull.

He moved into the living room, where the lower half of the body stretched across the threshold, the legs pointing towards the table in the middle of the room. Beyond the outstretched corpse the room was cluttered with china chamber pots, kettles and boxes, which contained items wrapped in brown paper, much of which was 'bespattered with blood'.[7] His attention shifted to the table in the middle of the room, itself piled high with a mix of household paraphernalia, but he particularly noticed a selection of crockery, an oil lamp, a cup and saucer which appeared to have the remnants of a cup of tea, and another which contained cocoa. A quarter of a loaf of bread lay next to a full pint bottle on the table. He sniffed it and knew immediately it was beer. He remembered last May when he had stood in the same room looking at a bottle of gin. Had she fallen over again and smashed her head on the way down? Possible, he thought. But what about the dead dog? How had that happened? He looked back at the weight on the floor and refocussed on the theory that she had been smashed over the head.

On the table, a bloodstained, broken-open packet containing nine boxes of matches stared up at him. More matches, more blood. Plates, cups, saucers and jars, all new, filled the rest of the table, and Kirby soon realised that, while the room looked untidy, this was obviously another storage area for the shop. In the far corner beneath the only window of the room, an armchair nestled next to a wall-mounted glass cabinet. Nothing to help him there. His increasingly enquiring stare moved slowly round the room and spotted a tin kettle on the hearth in front of the fire. A small clock occupied the space on the mantelpiece above it. As he made his way round to the other side of the body, he noticed that more tin kettles and chamber pots stacked neatly on the floor were covered in blood; one chamber pot was 'very much broken'. Along the wall next to the body, curtains hid shelving below another cabinet. This time, though, blood was splashed across the width of the glass frontage with more on the vertical upright of the door frame next to it. On the floor, a dog basket was pushed into the far left-hand corner.

Kirby took time to consider what he had seen so far. An apparently disorganised and cluttered room, a dead woman, a dead dog, and blood everywhere. He couldn't dismiss the 'drunken woman falling over' theory but was becoming more satisfied that this was foul play. Keen to get on with using his detective skills, he stepped out of the living room and moved to the foot of the stairs. He wasn't sure why, but he shouted out to see if anyone answered, but, getting no reply, he moved forward into the passageway which led to the front door of the shop, making another mental note of the shelves on the left-hand side neatly stacked with pots, saucepans, bowls, jugs, oil lamps and, hanging in abundance from the ceiling, more broom heads. He could now see the blind drawn fully down on the shop front door and, raising it to allow more light into the house, he saw that the door was secured by a spring lock and bolted in the locked position at the bottom. The killer didn't go out the front door then, he mumbled to himself as his confidence grew. A copy of the day's *Daily Mail* protruded through the letterbox, a shilling and two sixpenny pieces resting on the doormat beneath it, which was littered with splashes of candle grease. Once again, the coins had blood on them. On the passageway floor between the front door and the bodies rested a 'cardboard receptacle similar to those used for jam and treacle'. He picked it up, and looking closely he saw blood on its inside and outside. He put it back down again. With the extra light now shining through, he saw a trail of blood between Mrs Ridgley's body and the entrance to the converted front room.

Entering the shop, he followed the trail, which led to behind a counter on the other side of the room. A raised hatch gave access to where there were shelves from floor to ceiling packed with stock. There was no spare space, Mrs Ridgley catering for virtually every household need, from foodstuffs to cleaning materials, utensils to confectionery, children's toys, tools, coffee, tobacco, cigarettes and matches. An open drawer behind the counter, which Kirby quickly calculated to be the till, was covered in blood and contained a single farthing coin. There were more bloodspots on the counter, and he saw that the floor was covered with numerous packets of Woodbine cigarettes. A brass paraffin lamp above the counter was extinguished, but Kirby's eyes had adjusted sufficiently for him to see more boxes of matches strewn across the shop floor below the window. This was a classic murder scene if ever he had seen one. The shop had clearly been ransacked, money stolen and the shopkeeper and her dog bludgeoned to death using the four-pound weight. He was nervously excited.

He walked slowly up the stairs, examined each of the rooms, noting only that more candlewax appeared on the floor. Seeing that jewellery and other personal items appeared untouched, he went back downstairs, stepped over the dead dog and, much to his annoyance, trod in the excreta lying to its rear. Edwin Sutton, one of the neighbours who accompanied Constable Kirby into the house, was sure that the motion had already been trodden in when he first saw it and didn't think that the footprint had been caused by Kirby. It is a moot point. Annoyed with himself for being so careless, he stepped outside to dislodge the mess from his boot just as Sergeant Charles Boarder and the police surgeon, Dr William Grellett, appeared at the back gate. He was not only annoyed but now embarrassed.

The time was shortly before 11am, and despite his mishap, Kirby, pleased with his work so far, took great care in briefing his sergeant and the doctor on what he had discovered, and before they entered the house, he said to them both, 'Be careful, because it might turn out to be a case of murder.'

Kirby led them through to where Mrs Ridgley lay, and Grellett leaned over the body, frowning as he looked closely at the blood around her face. After a few seconds, the doctor directed the sergeant to drag the body from the hallway into the rear living room so that he could see in the better light. Kirby was confused. He knew that nothing should be disturbed and had spent the last half an hour making sure that as much as possible was left untouched. He looked on in horror as Boarder dragged Mrs Ridgley by her legs, revealing a pool of blood on the living room floor.

The doctor stepped forward to make a closer examination. Bloody wounds were now more visible at the back of the head, and in order to look more closely, he removed the garments which were wrapped around her neck – an apron loosely crossed over at the front in the form of a scarf and a khaki handkerchief which had been tied loosely in a knot at the back. Both were saturated in blood. With Kirby still looking on in amazement, the doctor rolled the body onto its side, revealing the arms that had been hidden underneath, and he saw that her hands were tightly clenched. He stood back from his examination, casually taking in the sight of some burnt matches on the floor by the door. He paused for thought, looking from the body to the police officers, and he drew breath. The woman, he announced, had been murdered.[8]

Satisfied that nothing more could be usefully done in the house, the doctor directed that the body be taken to the nearby St Saviour's mortuary. Kirby bristled with excitement, and with a spring in his step, he went next door to telephone the police station to tell them that Ridgley had been murdered and that an ambulance was required. He was told emphatically by the desk sergeant to make sure that the body wasn't moved. Inspectors Frederick Warren and Walter Bowyer were on their way.

Chapter 4

Learning His Trade

London, 1888

Apparently, the man they were looking for was a butcher, or perhaps a surgeon. Some had even suggested that he was a woman. The person would be covered in blood and certainly some sort of madman. He strangled prostitutes and then cut their bodies open, leaving their entrails on display, presumably designed to shock. Scotland Yard was being put under pressure to find the man the newspapers had dubbed 'Jack the Ripper', and even among the sleazy back streets of East London, people were running scared.

Frederick Porter Wensley was one of dozens of constables drafted into the area to keep watch at night for anything they thought would lead to the Ripper, though quite what they was looking for nobody knew. Wensley had only just enrolled earlier that year, a west-country boy, and now here he was looking out for Britain's biggest killer. It was dark, the streets dimly lit by the occasional gas lamp which gave brief glimpses of drunken women awkwardly being pushed up against grimy walls as men looked for a quick, cheap encounter. Drunks littered the pavements and ordinarily, Wensley would have either moved them on or arrested them. But he had been told to stay on the streets. Any one of these people could be the next victim, or the Ripper himself.

He decided to slide down one of the many narrow alleys that characterised Whitechapel. He had stuck rubber strips to the soles of his boots to allow a silent approach. He was an ambitious copper and had worked out that the killer was cleverer than most people were giving him credit for. He moved cautiously, silently, straining his eyes as the light dimmed the further he moved along, not wanting to use his lantern to give away his presence. Suddenly, something hard hit him in the face, and despite the strap, which was firmly under his chin, his helmet fell to the floor and Wensley instinctively fell to protect himself. Silence.

He heard no footsteps running away; he switched on his bullseye lantern and found himself staring at a pair of a man's boots at his head height. He shone his light upwards and made out the figure of a man hanging from a wooden beam overhead. Wensley blew his whistle.

Many teased young Wensley about the 'hanging man' for months to come, but like all young constables, he was learning his trade. He tangled with vicious and unscrupulous criminals and quickly got a reputation for making good arrests. His efforts were rewarded in 1895 when he was appointed to the Criminal Investigation Department (CID). Promotions followed and he was awarded the Kings Police Medal (KPM) in 1909.

It was the siege of Sidney Street that dominated the headlines in 1911. A month earlier in December a gang of Russian burglars had been disturbed in a jeweller's shop in Houndsditch. At a time when firearms were rare in London, three police officers had been shot dead and the killers had got away. Several arrests were made but two members of the gang were holed up at No 100 Sidney Street and were surrounded by armed police. A gun battle ensued during which Wensley, who was directing operations, narrowly missed death bullets as they passed close to his head; the *Evening News* even announced his death. The situation was so dangerous, that the Home Secretary, Winston Churchill, who had already ordered the Scots Guards and the Royal Horse Artillery to the scene, turned up. The Russians set fire to the house; one was killed by the police, the other dying as a result of smoke inhalation. When Wensley entered the gutted building, the ceiling collapsed, killing the fireman standing next to him.

If that wasn't enough pressure, in the first hours of the siege Wensley was also actively engaged in a murder investigation, assisting one of his colleagues after the discovery of a man who had just been found brutally murdered on Clapham Common. The effect of all this was to seriously affect his health and he was granted compassionate leave. Sir Melville Macnaghten, the head of Scotland Yard's CID at the time, wrote:

'Detective Inspector Wensley has been hopelessly overworked for the last three months and is perilously near a breakdown. I cannot speak in sufficiently high terms of the work he has done and I strongly recommend that he be granted special leave for fourteen days.'

The commissioner of the Metropolitan Police, Sir Edward Henry, endorsed the report:

> 'I entirely concur. I will sanction as much special leave in excess of fourteen days as may be required, so that Mr Wensley may have a real good rest.'

The overworked detective went home and spent two relaxing weeks with his wife and children.

Wensley's memoirs refer to a variety of bizarre cases including one in which he and a colleague, under cover as officers of the Royal Horse Artillery, got into trouble investigating an illegal gambling den. Uniformed men burst in and Wensley threw himself across the table to prevent the cash being whisked away. One of the criminals grabbed Wensley's riding crop from him and had thrashed him mercilessly. Despite Wensley quickly declaring that he was a police officer, the beating continued. He was unable to sit down for several days.

He had developed into quite a sardonic-looking man with a cool, almost offhand, manner set off by his high collar and shrewd eyes. He boasted a thin, angular, very Jewish-looking face with bright piercing eyes that bored into you, matched with slow and hesitant speech. He had no pretensions, and his simple object in life was to get at the truth of the cases he was charged with investigating, and it was this simplicity of outlook, combined with great resolution and a complete absence of fear, which made him one of the great detectives. He was a workaholic, expecting the same from everyone he supervised. He maintained strong discipline and dress sense, expecting his men always to act and dress like gentlemen; the wearing of braces was most important. Yet, he was one of the few men who never wanted to work at Scotland Yard, not wishing to move from his beloved East End of London where he lived, had always worked, and where the criminals glibly referred to him as the Weasel, in reference to the Jewish version on his name, Wenzel. His fellow officers referred to him – behind his back of course – as the Elephant, on account of his long nose. It was routine, when an officer was promoted to the rank of detective chief inspector, as he was in 1912, to be transferred to the Yard, but such was his knowledge of the East End, that upon his promotion he was allowed to remain. Tragedy struck though in 1916, when his close friend and colleague, Detective Chief Inspector Alfred Ward, was suddenly killed in a zeppelin bomb raid. Wensley was appointed as his replacement and transferred to the Yard's murder squad.

Murder was now his business.

Chapter 5

A Theory Emerges

Hertfordshire, Monday, 27 January 1919

It was now 11.15 am, almost an hour since Kirby had found the body. Inspectors Warren and Bowyer listened to the constable as he outlined what he had done and seen. Everything was covered in blood, he emphasised, his excitement barely contained. The two senior officers looked at the body in its new position in the living room and the doctor told of the blood he had found to the back of the victim's head. They walked around the house seeing for themselves the disarray that Kirby had described. Warren had seen all he needed to see for now, and in the absence of his superintendent, who was in London, he agreed the bodies could be moved. Kirby could do that and Sergeant Boarder could take the dog; someone would need to have a look at the carcase. The ambulance arrived, Elizabeth Ridgley was conveyed to the hospital with Kirby and PC 269 Bignell on board and the dog was despatched to the veterinary surgeon. The only officer who had made a detailed examination of the scene had been sent away, and within two and half hours of him finding the body, it had been removed.

The two inspectors now set about their work. Bowyer saw everything that Kirby had briefed him on, the bloodstaining throughout the ground floor, particularly the chest-height spattering on the glass cabinet, but, unlike Kirby, he didn't notice the blood on the broken china chamber pot. He made a specific point of examining the four-pound weight, which his constable had pointed out to him and 'was absolutely certain that there was no human hair on it' though 'there were some sandy hairs corresponding with the colour of the dog'.[9] He turned his attention to the shop in the front room of the house and, as he examined the counter, he too saw the blood spots and smears near the raised hatch, on the counter near the till drawer, in the drawer itself and on the floor immediately below.

He stepped outside and spoke to Annie Withey, who had presented herself at the shop door and told him that she had seen Mrs Ridgley outside her shop around 8.30pm on the night of Saturday, 25 January, when she had a conversation with her about buying an oak tray. The woman told the inspector that the grocer appeared happy.[10]

Inside, Inspector Warren was rather more thorough, enumerating the items on the ground floor: fourteen kettles; twelve saucepans; three enamel chambers; eleven earthenware chamber pots; a quantity of scrubbing brushes; broom heads and, unlike his fellow inspector, he made a specific note of 'a broken earthenware chamber'.[11] Many were wrapped in brown paper and the majority were covered in blood, particularly a chamber pot situated on the floor underneath the living room table, which contained sufficient blood to cover the bottom of the container. There was blood trailing from the living room door to the glass cabinet. He stood among the piles of merchandise, which practically filled the room, the bloodstained utensils and the cracked chamber pot, and started to develop his ideas. Messy, he thought, but there were no signs of any struggle.

It was his turn now to move into the shop, where he saw the same bloodstains and smears spoken of by Constable Kirby, but again he came to the conclusion that there had been no struggle. The house was admittedly cluttered, although he too thought that it was something of an organised mess, the sign of a busy shopkeeper, but nothing suggested to him that there had been any violence. He returned to the four-pound weight, something that couldn't be ignored, and examined it. It was covered in blood and had 'ginger hairs' on it, which he thought resembled coconut matting, but they weren't, he surmised, human. No, still no signs of any struggle or violence. He finished with a casual look, which revealed nothing out of the ordinary, and he had seen all he needed to see.

Outside, he looked at the rear gate which Kirby had clambered over with the neighbours and was sure that marks on the surface were consistent with their entry into the back garden.

Other neighbours were by now standing in Garden Row watching the police go about their business. Louisa Roach lived and worked as a bootseller immediately next door to Mrs Ridgley and shared the adjoining wall. She got the inspector's attention and told him that between 8pm and 9pm on Saturday she had heard Mrs Ridgley's dog barking loudly, which was followed by two or three 'thuds' and the dog then appeared to groan twice. She eventually went to bed, she said, around 11.15pm, but at midnight she heard some moaning, which went on for about two hours before eventually getting fainter. Assuming the noise was coming from another neighbour's house, she looked out of the window, saw nothing and went back to bed.

Warren listened and asked if she had heard any scuffling but she replied she hadn't.[12] A similar story emerged from another neighbour on the opposite side of Garden Row, who said that at about 1.30am on the Sunday morning his wife had woken him and said she too had heard a thud. She assumed that the noise came from soldiers who were billeting with them, shouted out, and, getting no response, went back to bed.[13]

Warren was pleased with himself. His close interrogation of witnesses had given a clearer picture of events.[14] He knew that Mrs Ridgley was alive and well at around 8.30pm on Saturday and that strange thudding noises were heard in or near the house shortly after that. And now here she was, dead, with apparent head injuries. No, thought Warren, still nothing to suggest any violence, and, assured that nothing was untoward, he headed for the mortuary to join his colleagues.

Boarder had already taken the dead dog to the veterinary surgery of William Goldsmith in Bridge Street, and having explained the circumstances in which the dog was found, and because of the froth found around its mouth, both he and Kirby thought that perhaps the animal had been poisoned. The vet had taken some samples and said he had let the police know in due course. The sergeant then joined his colleagues at the mortuary.

Dr William Pennington Grellett was an experienced medical practitioner who had performed many examinations and post mortems in cases of sudden and unexplained deaths. He carefully removed the bloodstained apron and the handkerchief, which was wrapped around the dead woman's neck, and then, between them, the police officers removed and searched Mrs Ridgley's remaining clothing, which both Warren and Bowyer commented, 'were not disarranged or torn'.[15] Inspector Warren again listed the articles and contents as they were removed from the body:

'1 skirt with 5½d in bronze coins in pocket (large quantity of blood on front near bottom)
1 pair of corsets (no blood)
1 woman's vest (smear of blood on back of neck)
1 pair of bloomers (no blood)
1 pair of combinations (smear of blood on neck at back)
1 petticoat (smear of blood at bottom at back)
1 bodice (large quantity of blood at neck, breast and arms)
1 under-bodice (spots of blood on neck and front)
1 apron (saturated in blood – found round neck)
1 khaki handkerchief found round neck (saturated in blood)

1 leather belt (no blood)
1 pair of lace-up boots (one very small spot on outside of left
boot on toe cap)'

Warren commented that the spot on the boot was hardly discernible with the eye.

The body now naked, Grellett resumed his examination. He scrutinised the injuries to the head and saw that, below Ridgley's mouth on her chin, and towards the left, there was a one-inch horizontal lacerated wound. Both eyelids were contused, but the right one was more swollen than the left, and on the bridge of the nose was a small wound about an eighth of an inch long. More were to be found on her left scalp, at the base of the cranium and at the top of the spine, which penetrated to the bone. To the left of this was an angular cut adjacent to a two-inch wound, which also extended to the bone. On the helix of the right ear was a wound about an inch long, of which the skin surrounding it had been 'torn up.'[16] His work finished, he turned to the two inspectors as if looking for some opinion from them, given that they too had been to the house and seen where Mrs Ridgley had been found.

The two inspectors looked at each other in turn, pouted their lips and shrugged their shoulders. Kirby glared at them both, his glance shifting nervously between his bosses and the doctor. Surely someone was going to say something about how this poor woman had been killed? This was murder, wasn't it?

The two inspectors, though, seemed rather more concerned with meeting their superintendent, who, they'd been told, was on his way to Nightingale Road. Almost oblivious to the reason why the police were witnessing an examination of a woman found dead in her house, they thanked the doctor and headed back. Kirby and, to a lesser degree, Grellett were confused. What was the next step? The doctor started to tidy up the mess and Kirby left the hospital with Sergeant Boarder.

At the same time, at quarter past five, some seven hours since Mrs Ridgley's body had been found, Superintendent George Reed arrived at the shop. He was now in charge.

Chapter 6

County Kerry, Ireland

Listowel, 1916

John Healy returned to life in rural Ireland and found the village of Clievragh easy enough to adapt to after the Western Front. This was his home, where he had grown up, had attended the Listowel Convent Infant and National School, worked on the farms and at the age of seventeen joined the army. He now moved back into the family home, a house in a corner of a field, where his father looked after his cows. His mother, Mary, had died six years earlier, having been diagnosed by the local medical practitioner as 'positively insane' and would have been admitted to a lunatic asylum many years before had his father not prevented it.[17] Four brothers and his youngest sister still lived there, but other siblings had long since moved on.[18]

Employment was hard to find during the war, but Healy found work as a farm labourer in nearby Listowel. It wasn't long though before he started to drink heavily, and he would often go for long walks, making rambling statements about the war.[19] Everyone had known John before he was called up for military service, and the insanity in his family was well known, but he was generally regarded, at least by his employer, as honest and industrious. But as his drinking became worse, he picked arguments with his fellow workmen, attacking them and taking out his apparent anger on the horses, whipping them unmercifully without reason. Healy seemed unable to control his outbursts, so the farmer had sacked him, but Healy begged for his job back. Despite the farmer still regarding him as unbalanced, he reluctantly agreed to take him back; after all, he was a war hero.[20]

But there was no let-up in his habits. After work, he went to the pubs in Listowel drinking whatever money he had and got back home in the evenings where, fuelled with beer, he took out his anger on his family. He punched his father in the face, fought with his brothers, threatened to burn the house down and threw his younger sister back into the house when through sheer fear she had tried to escape. He became so violent that the police were called, and they were confronted by a family all fighting with each other and one of the brothers smashing John on the head with a set of tongs to try and calm him down. All the windows in the house were smashed and bloodied bodies lay everywhere. So concerned were the police about the extraordinary level of violence that they called two of the local doctors to examine the family. They considered that one of the brothers, Thomas, was as 'mad as a March hare and needed to be put in an asylum'. John, in particular, was 'excitable, of hasty temper and self-conceited.'[21] The police agreed: 'all the Healy boys [were] strange in their manner'.[22]

Increasingly, the war veteran was finding it more and more difficult to adjust to post-war life, and his constant confrontations with the police were making him angry. For two years since leaving the army he had struggled, and he now decided that a new life was needed. He packed a bag and set off for England; apparently there was plenty of work there for Irish labourers. He was right, and he found himself a job as a labourers' supervisor in Lincolnshire. It didn't last long. No sooner had he started than he was quickly dismissed for negligence.[23] Disillusioned, he returned to Ireland during the summer of 1918, but now his attentions towards beer and violence were tempered by his attraction to a woman in the town, someone he had known before he had gone to war. He started seeing Hannah Dore, known as Annie, and on 13 August they married. But Healy had made another decision as well. He had no intention of staying in Ireland and needed a permanent change. He now had a wife, and he set his sights once again on England.

Chapter 7

The Theory Develops

Hertfordshire, Monday, 27 January 1919

George Reed had been a police officer since 1887 and had now been appointed by the chief constable as the officer in charge of Hitchin police district. He was a local man, kind and caring, who had been born into a farming family in Goose Green, near Hoddesdon and, at the age of sixteen, had joined the 7th Queen's Own Light Dragoons (Hussars). He had been part of the expeditionary force which was sent to relieve General Gordon at Khartoum in 1884, and been engaged in skirmishes on the River Nile and after the battle of Abu Klea in 1885; for both he had been awarded war medals.

Married the year after he had joined the Hertfordshire Constabulary, he had four daughters and had gone on to have a varied career including regularly guarding Edward VII on his many visits to the Rothschild family at Tring Park. Over the years, he had been often favourably commented upon in the local newspapers, outlining many of his successes at apprehending criminals. He had been congratulated for capturing a fraudster who had escaped to France, clearing up a burglary at a local hotel and locating and arresting a man wanted for numerous offences of dishonesty throughout the county. And when the townspeople of Hitchin rioted for two days in protest at the increase in food prices just after the outbreak of war in 1914, it was Reed who had commanded his officers and controlled a very nasty situation. Shopkeepers and their premises were attacked, and he appealed to the better nature of the protestors, who agreed to disperse, a difficult task since many were from the labouring classes who were suffering oppressive working conditions and miserable housing in slums. War and poverty had become a dangerous mix.

His exposure to murder investigations, though, was somewhat limited, and he remembered well an investigation he had been in charge of six years earlier in 1913, which resulted in disastrous consequences. He had been well acquainted with an ongoing neighbourly dispute in nearby Letchworth, which, despite his attempts to reconcile the differences between the two, resulted in one shooting the other dead. The killer walked into the police station and announced, 'Well Mr Reed, I have shot Bell.' The superintendent attended the house, recovered the firearm and proceeded to remove the bullets from it to make it safe. However, in handling the weapon, he discharged a bullet which shot through his left hand, ricocheted off the building and plunged itself into the stomach of a somewhat inquisitive neighbour curious as to the police presence. One man dead, another one injured, and a superintendent with a self-inflicted wound.

Although his plan had been to retire in 1914, the war had prevented that, with reservists being called up, forcing officers beyond retirement age to remain in service, and he stayed in post to oversee policing in the town. With the war now over, retirement once again loomed, and he was looking forward to it. For the time being though, he had a job to do, and he was greeted by the two inspectors at the door of 125 Nightingale Road. He listened to them as they outlined the injuries to the dead woman and the dog, the helpful information they'd already obtained from the neighbours, and how Kirby had needed to rescue the woman from the house the year before. Daylight by now had completely disappeared and the dark made it difficult for Reed to be able to see anything in the house, but by the aid of a lighted candle and a magnifying glass he perused the scene, Warren and Bowyer following. The two inspectors tried to point out the pots and pans and where Ridgely had been found, but it was a thankless task. Reed gave in to the darkness and decided to come back the next day. There was no rush.

The following morning, together with Inspector Bowyer and Constable Kirby, who was keen to impress upon his high-ranking boss his thoughts about this being a murder, the superintendent walked through the house, this time helped by the daylight. Everything downstairs seemed to fit with what he had been told. A large pool of blood, about a quarter of a pint,[24] in a bedroom chamber pot resting on the living room floor captured his attention, and more appeared to be liberally splattered throughout the living room, passageway and shop. The floor where the body had been found was littered with Ridgley's stock, and he saw for himself the large numbers of kettles, saucepans, earthenware, tin-ware and bedroom chambers he had been told about. As he viewed the mess, he thought about the injuries to Mrs Ridgley and also considered the likely poisoning of the Irish terrier. What was the scene telling him?

As he walked around the ground floor, shifting and picking up items to inspect, he took in the image of this corner shop, which had no electricity or gas and was lit only by candles and paraffin lamps hanging from the ceiling, on the living room table and one he saw sitting on a mantelpiece in the kitchen. They were all extinguished, but each had ample oil and wick and were capable of being lit. He scanned from the rear window in the living room through to the front door and shop area. Any light, he thought, emitted from the lamps in the shop would have been dim and would scarcely have been visible from the street outside due to the well-stocked front window. Certainly, he calculated, the light from the lamp in the living room wouldn't have been visible from outside due to the blind on the front door being drawn down and heavy curtains in the living room, which had been drawn when Kirby had found the body. As for the lamp in the kitchen, if this had been lit at any time only a dim light would have been seen, given its distance from Garden Row and the high hedgerow which blocked the view. The lamps fascinated him, and he lifted them up to have a better look, after which he satisfied himself that there was no evidence of any smoke residue in the chimneys.[25] He put the lamps down and carried on with his search.

The indefatigable Kirby, displaying a deal of deference to his superintendent, drew his attention to the used matches on the living room floor where Mrs Ridgley's body had rested. Reed nodded. He bent down to make a closer examination of the utensils on the floor, which revealed the presence of some hairs and three hairpins lying on the floor beside them. Keen to impress, Kirby reminded him about the four-pound weight and the cigar box which he had found in the passageway close to the body; both appeared to have blood on them.

As if reacting to being told what to do by a junior officer, Reed picked up the weight, looked at it, and put it back on the floor. He said nothing, and Bowyer glared at the constable. Reed was already forming an opinion. After all, he did have thirty-two years police service behind him. Now that he was here, everything was under control.

Reprimand aside, Kirby was now having the opportunity to see the premises in daylight for a second time, and he made a more detailed inspection of the shop and living accommodation. He was enjoying himself. He looked behind the living room door and found two unlocked wooden sweet boxes and a tin box. He opened the wooden boxes and saw books and correspondence, which, on closer examination, revealed that they related to the shop's takings and accounts. Inside the tin box, he found envelopes, each containing cash, which when he added it all up came to £3.9s.6d in silver and £4 in Treasury notes. He cast his attention further around the room and found another wooden box, which he opened and discovered a number of purses with more cash inside. This time there was £2.1s.6d with a few loose farthings in the box. Kirby's keen eye was equally attracted to the bloodstained glass cabinet in the room and through the glass he saw a collection of handkerchiefs. Remembering that a handkerchief was found around the neck of the dead woman, he opened the cabinet and took them out. There were three of them and they looked new, and it seemed likely they were items that would be sold in the shop. He drew this find and the money behind the door to the attention of his superintendent, who was busy exploring the shop with its blood and cigarettes spread all over the floor. Reed almost dismissively listened to Kirby's news but was more interested in having a look upstairs. He motioned for Kirby to take the lead.

As the Hertfordshire police officers went up the stairs, Kirby pointed out the deposit of candlewax on the landing floor to his superiors. Again, Reed nodded. The front room appeared to be a sitting room. Another was being used as a storeroom, and they focussed their efforts on Mrs Ridgley's bedroom at the back. Together, they searched an open drawer in a dresser, which had a bag resting on the top alongside an open empty purse and a gold ring in a case. The other drawers contained nothing of particular interest, and Kirby opened a large oak storage chest in which, after ferreting through a quantity of gentleman's clothing and various papers, he found a woman's silver watch, another purse and a paper bag containing a further £5.17s.6d.[26] In all, he had now found just over £15.8s.11d.

Reed instructed that the mattress on the bed be lifted, and once it had been pulled back by Kirby and Bowyer, a lady's gold watch, chain and gold ring in a jewel case were revealed. The superintendent thought carefully about what the upstairs was telling him. No obvious signs of a disturbance, candlewax on the floor, no traces of any blood anywhere and a large amount of cash and jewellery in places not difficult to find. He now decided that he had seen all he needed to see and left for the mortuary, leaving instructions with Bowyer and Kirby to try and trace the relatives of the deceased. On the way out, he picked up the four-pound weight.

With the weight, now resting on the mortuary table, and the apron and handkerchief on a nearby table, which had been removed the day before by Dr Grellett, the superintendent listened. The police surgeon itemised the injuries to the body, making it plain that the deceased had a number of cut wounds to the back of her head, the bridge of her nose was broken and she had three slight wounds to the face: one over the right eye; one on the left cheek; and one on the jaw.[27] Although it was possible for some of the injuries to have been caused by falling on the kettles and chamber pots, this was, in his view, a clear case of murder.[28] The superintendent thanked him for his opinion and headed back to the police station.

He took the weight with him.

Chapter 8

Irish Life in Hitchin

November 1918

No 3, Ickleford Road, Hitchin would do. The lodgings were close enough to where he had found employment at Andersons in Henlow as a labourer and there were other Irish people in the house. John and Annie Healy, the newly married couple from Listowel, would be okay here for a while. His wages were just about enough, £3.8s.6d a week, and the rent was affordable. It was November 1918, the war had finished and he was well away from all that now. It was a small, mid-terrace house, less than a five-minute walk away from the centre of town and, as a bonus, a number of public houses were within a short walking distance.

The spinster landlady, Catherine Lawrence, wasn't quite so pleased. The Irish couple had arrived, and very quickly she saw, in Healy, a man with a violent temper. All had been okay at first, but one morning, Healy had risen late for work, probably hungover from the night before, and she suggested to him, quite innocently, that perhaps his alarm clock hadn't gone off because he had accidentally touched the hands.

He flew into a violent temper, his wiry, yet athletic figure bending above her. 'If you'd been a man, I would bash your brains in,' he shouted.

She became wary, though not scared, and for a while the Irishman seemed amiable enough, although she noticed that his wife deferred to him. She also quickly realised that Annie Healy never had any money and had occasion to ask her landlady whether she could borrow six shillings. When she had later tried to get Annie to pay back some of the money, Healy overheard and flew into a temper. Towering above her, he shouted, 'You're worse than the beasts in the field. I'll crush you and anyone who stands in my way.'

Lawrence stood her ground. 'It's no use you murdering me, as you'll get no money,' she blasted back.

Healy frequently quarrelled with his young wife, and Lawrence watched speechless as he made his wife sit opposite him and with his face up close to hers, said, 'You grow more and more like your mother every day. How I hate her.'

It wasn't long before Lawrence, alone in the house with Healy, was subjected to more violent threats. Again, she stood up to him. 'You are no man to threaten a woman and call her such names when she's in the house by herself. There is a God above you, and I don't think I'll go by your hands.'

Alarmed, Healy backed off. But she was fed up with the aggravation. They had to go. She couldn't stand it any longer and asked them to move out; and just before Christmas they did. She was hardly surprised, when, a few weeks later, on 15 January, Mrs Ridgley from the grocer's shop on the corner of Garden Row and Nightingale Road called on her looking for the Healys. They both used her shop and now owed her money, but although Lawrence didn't know their new address, she made a suggestion.

'You shouldn't be afraid of that man Healy. Next time he comes into the shop, confront him. Don't be put off just because he's a violent man.'[29]

Mrs Ridgley thought that a good idea. She would do just that.

Chapter 9

A Folly

The coroner, Mr Francis Shillitoe, opened the inquest into the death of Mrs Elizabeth Ridgley on Tuesday, 28 January 1919, at the St Saviour's Vicar's Room, Hitchin. As was routine, the purpose of the initial inquest hearing was to establish the identity of the deceased and to consider the prima facie cause of death.

Among the items brought into court to assist was the khaki handkerchief found around the neck of Mrs Ridgley, and Superintendent Reed outlined the finding of the bodies. The deceased's sister, Mrs Mary Chandler, and her husband, John, had been located at their south London address and had arrived the night before and now attended the inquest together with Mrs Roach and Dr Grellett. Chandler told the hearing that she had identified the deceased as that of her sister, a widower, and that she was fifty-four years of age.[30] Louisa Roach retold her story of hearing Mrs Ridgley's dog between 8.20pm and 9pm on the evening of Saturday, 25 January, although she now described what she heard as the dog barking 'furiously', followed by a loud thud. At midnight, she thought she heard groans and got out of bed on three occasions to investigate, albeit by only looking out of her bedroom window. She heard no signs of any struggle and came to the conclusion that one of her neighbours was ill.

Dr Grellett detailed the injuries he had seen on Mrs Ridgley's body, specifically those to the face and the back of her head and which were consistent with her having stood up after an initial fall only to fall over again. He told the coroner that he was shown several bloodstained items at the scene, including the cash drawer in the shop, some coins found at the front door and, importantly, a four-pound weight which had been found close to the body and which in his opinion could have been used to have inflict the injuries. The bottom of the weight bore hairs similar to Mrs Ridgley's.

Mr Shillitoe asked the doctor, 'Could the wounds have been caused by her defending herself against an attack by a dog?'

Grellett replied, 'No. I think she was very fond of the dog.'

'Could the wounds have been self-inflicted?' the coroner persisted.

'No, certainly not,' came the doctor's emphatic reply.

Superintendent Reed then retook his place in the makeshift witness stand. However, he merely informed the hearing that a great deal of money had been found on the premises and there was no evidence that any money was missing. He needed more time, he said, for the police to carry out their enquiries and to search the premises more thoroughly.

The short hearing finished quickly, and Shillitoe summarised in a few words the evidence that had been presented. The dead woman was Mrs Elizabeth Ridgley, she was found, together with her dead dog, in her heavily bloodstained shop, with substantial head injuries, which by implication could have been caused by the four-pound weight found close to her body. Whatever took place happened on the evening of Saturday, 25 January. The deceased's injuries were not consistent with being attacked by her dog, it was not a suicide, and robbery did not appear to be the motive. As nothing else was forthcoming, the coroner adjourned the matter until 19 February.

As he reached forward to endorse his decision, his hand accidentally knocked over a bottle of ink, and PC Kirby, instinctively and in an effort to assist, picked up the nearest item he could find to mop up the spillage. His face, and that of the coroner, turned to shock as they both realised that the constable had grabbed the bloodstained khaki handkerchief to clean the surface.[31] Not only bloodstained, but now heavily ink-stained. For the second time, Kirby was annoyed with himself.

The following day, Reed went back to the mortuary with Dr Grellett where he discussed with him the different possibilities of the cause of death. Grellett listened to the senior policeman and decided to perform a more detailed examination on Mrs Ridgley. This revealed that the base of the skull was fractured, which may, he concurred with the superintendent, have been caused by falling or as a result of a blow from somebody else but confirmed that the cause of death was a fractured skull and consequent brain haemorrhage.[32]

Reed looked at the body on the slab, turned his gaze towards the doctor and, once again, thanked him. As he walked out of St Saviour's hospital he made his own assessment. These injuries, he thought, confirmed everything he had seen at the shop. But he needed to make another visit first – this time to the veterinary surgeon.

Inside the surgery, Reed stood before Goldsmith, weight in hand. Ridgley 'may have been knocked about' he said, and he asked the surgeon to look at the dog again to see if he could see any injuries.

Not looking for evidence of poisoning anymore, Goldsmith looked more closely at the head, parting the hair and making careful incisions into the back of the skull. The skin was discoloured and he told Reed that this was bruising, extensive bruising, in fact, on the front of the skull and behind the ears.

Reed looked at him in a manner designed to make the surgeon say more.

The injuries, he said, effectively amounted to a 'blow at the back of the head' and must have been inflicted 'by two or three exceedingly heavy blows by a powerful person and with a blunt instrument.' The skull wasn't fractured though.[33]

Reed handed him the four-pound weight and asked, 'Could that have done it? Do you think that's what caused the injuries?'

Goldsmith looked at the lump of iron, held it against the skull of the dog and looked back at the weight. Reed waited patiently. Eventually Goldsmith spoke. 'I do not think it could have been done by the four-pound weight.'[34]

For the third time, the superintendent thanked a medical man for his opinion and informed him that the carcase of the dog may now be destroyed. Now, with the knowledge of what he had been told about the injuries to the dog and having spoken in more detail to Dr Grellett and had the benefit of looking closely at the scene, Reed's theory was forming.[35] He could explain exactly what had happened and he made his way back to the police station to compile his report.

Reed sat at his desk with his pencil in hand, thinking. He was in serious mood, something which was reflected by his tunic still tightly buttoned up to his neck, his superintendent insignia prominently displayed on the collar. He was proud of his appearance and expected the same from his men and the thought of removing his tunic didn't cross his mind. His cap rested on the table and he stared at it, his fingers gently stroking his neatly-trimmed, greying moustache. When he smiled, his high cheekbones stood out from his rounded face giving a rather handsome appearance, but he was not in a smiling mood. His ideas were developing in his head and he started to write.

He based his thoughts on everything he had learned from the four witnesses that had been found: Gertrude Day, who first raised the alarm; Annie Withey who had seen Mrs Ridgley the evening before; Louisa Roach, who had heard the noises coming from the shop on the evening of 25 January; and the close neighbour of the deceased who had gone into the shop with PC Kirby and found the body. He had also now had the opportunity of speaking to Mary Chandler, the sister of the deceased, who told him that Elizabeth had been a reserved woman of uncertain temperament and that her dog was generally regarded by the neighbours as vicious. The shop business, though, was flourishing, her average weekly takings about £23 a week,[36] and because she didn't have a bank account, there was always plenty of money on the premises.

He reminded himself of what Kirby, Bowyer and Warren had told him and considered the opinion of Goldsmith, the veterinary surgeon, and Dr Grellett, the police surgeon. His own observations from the scene were spinning around inside his head. He outlined the injuries to Elizabeth Ridgley, those to her Irish terrier, Prince, and concluded that the animal was killed by a 'blow to the back of the head.'[37] Insofar as Mrs Ridgley was concerned, this was an unfortunate and dreadful accident.

Relying on his observations from the house, he thought about the cluttered darkness in which the deceased had lived. The paraffin lamps occupied his mind, and the fact they'd not been used suggested to him that the shopkeeper probably never used them, preferring to rely on candles. Candlewax all over the floors confirmed that. He felt very pleased with himself working this out and recalled also how the woman last year had stumbled around the house, probably with plenty of gin inside her, and almost burned to death when she had fallen on one of the paraffin lamps. By the looks of it, she had done the same again; had plenty of beer to drink, tripped up in the dark and smashed her head on the way down. Only this time there was no paraffin lamp to catch fire. Not wanting to cast the poor widow in a bad light though, he settled on a more sensitive conclusion. On the evening of 25 January, he wrote, in the dark of her house, the fifty-four-year-old grocer fell on the utensils in the living room and all her injuries were consistent with this. The pointed spouts of the kettles, handles of the saucepans and the broken earthenware chamber pot were sufficient to cause all the injuries. After lying for some time on the utensils, she then recovered sufficiently to be able to crawl or walk about three yards before collapsing in the spot where she was eventually found. There was blood on the floor which indicated her track between the utensils and her final resting place.

That concluded, he knew now that he needed to concern himself with all the other blood spattered and smeared around the shop, including spots found on the armchair in the far corner of the living room and on a broom handle resting against it. He was equally aware that drops of blood lay along the passageway between where the body was found and the front door, obviously 'where it had dripped from some person on to the floor'. He continued:

> 'There was blood on the bolt at the bottom of the front door which indicated that some person, either deceased or someone else, walked to the front door and handled the bolt with blood on their hands and bolted the door or attempted to unbolt it.'

Conscious of other blood leading from the passageway into the shop, drops and smears on the counter, in the till drawer and on the chair behind the counter, he further concluded that 'the person who walked to the front door and into the shop was evidently bleeding.' Finally, he stated that there was no blood upstairs and the blood on the floor between the body and the back door was as a result of the blood-saturated body being carried out that way by the police.

The blood on the four-pound weight next to the body troubled him, as Mary Chandler had told him that normally it would be kept with the scales in the scullery. At this point, Reed started to develop his theory about Mrs Ridgley stumbling in the dark and posited that:

> 'It is possible that the injuries to the face of deceased were also caused by a fall or she may have been struck in the face and knocked on her back falling onto the articles in the room. Mrs Ridgley may have first fallen over something or over the dog injuring her face. After doing this, she may have walked about, and the blood already mentioned in shop and passage may have come from her face. It is possible she may have killed the dog either with the weight or broom and after this may have fallen again, which caused the injuries to her head.'

He then applied his mind to the money on the premises. He pointed out that the cigar box found close to Mrs Ridgley's body and a treacle tin found in the passageway were normally kept in the till drawer. Further, two shillings in silver were found at the foot of the front door, and from this he deduced that Mrs Ridgley may have had the coins in her hand when she fell and that consequently 'there is no evidence that a robbery has taken place'. Reed supported this theory by identifying that Mrs Ridgley's routine was to keep her daily takings in the cigar box and treacle tin in the till drawer and at the end of each day carry the takings through to the living room, count them and enter the details in a memorandum book. Daily takings were entered, he said, in the book up until 24 January, but none was entered for 25 January, the day Mrs Ridgley probably died. A typical day's taking for a Saturday was about £10, and in the wooden boxes behind the living room door was, he inaccurately recorded, £12.5s.1½d, a figure rather more than Constable Kirby had said he had found. Reed's implication was that Mrs Ridgley died before she could enter the details in her book. She had no bank account and dealt only in cash.

Having covered all the points that he felt were important, the confident superintendent started to conclude his report. He argued 'that it is very difficult to judge whether Mrs Ridgley was killed by some person or if the injuries were all caused by falling. Although the dog appears to have been ferocious to strangers, he was practically blind.' He went on to say that the apron and khaki handkerchief, the latter of which was from her own stock, was put around her neck by Mrs Ridgley herself for the purpose of stopping the bleeding.

Satisfied he had explained everything, he finished by stating that the inquest had been adjourned until 19 February and that 'every possible enquiry has been made and up to now I can gain no information as to any person, other than the usual customers being seen near the premises.'[38]

The superintendent was happy with his report and retired for the evening.

Chapter 10

The Evidence is Buried

George Kirby, one of the town's undertakers and no relation to the constable excited about the murder he had discovered, had known Mrs Ridgley for some time, as he lived close to her shop and paid regular visits there for his groceries. He had been called to the mortuary by Dr Grellett after the post mortem to transfer the body to his funeral parlour, and on Saturday, 1 February, five days after she had been found dead, Elizabeth Ridgley made her final journey. The coffin, which was adorned with several wreaths of flowers, was followed by three carriages containing the principal mourners, Miss E. J. Gordon, Mr G. Gordon, Mrs Wilson, Mrs E. Eades, Mrs Pollard, Mr H. Gordon, Mrs M. A. Chandler, Miss R. Chandler, Mr J. Chandler and Mrs Gilbert, and as it wended its way through the snow-lined streets of Hitchin, small groups of people appeared, removing their headgear as a mark of respect, one stepping forward to take a photograph as it passed close by to Mrs Ridgley's shop. At midday, the cortege arrived at St Saviour's church, where the Reverend J.G. Williams conducted the service, Mrs Ridgley's relatives quietly mourning the unexplained death of their loved one. Half an hour later, the coffin was lowered into an unassuming grave in Hitchin cemetery and the gathering departed. The following day, Mary Chandler and her husband, John, who had been at the funeral and still in a state of grief, turned up at Hitchin police station at the request of Superintendent Reed. He wanted to finalise matters, and they now arrived, wondering what would be said. Reed was in a confident but respectful mood as he sat opposite them in his office at the police station, and he confirmed in great detail how their sister had suffered an unfortunate death and how doubly unfortunate it was that her dog had so unluckily died the same day due to the involuntary actions of Mrs Ridgley. They sat in silence listening to the most senior officer in charge of Hitchin police station explaining his theory. Having explained his findings, Reed opened an envelope, poured the contents onto the table and handed over £17.2s.7d in cash to them. He also gave them some boxes of correspondence, including the cash memorandum book, and told them that the shop was now being released from the police

36

and they should feel free to carry on with business as usual. Mary Chandler thanked the superintendent and returned to her sister's shop.

Reed could now submit his final report, and he sat down in front of his typewriter to fill in all the gaps and clarify any outstanding matters. He began by reiterating the injuries to Mrs Ridgley and emphasised that the base of the skull had been fractured, which may have been caused by falling or from a blow by someone else. Either way, the cause of death was a fractured skull and brain haemorrhage, but he 'can find no evidence to suggest that the woman was murdered'.[39] Given the positioning of the blood-spattering on the dead woman's blouse and apron, he stated that she must have been in an upright position when the blood fell on her but commented that due to an absence of blood on her back or undergarments, the cut to the back of her head couldn't have been made when in that position. As for the earthenware chamber pot with blood inside it, the deceased must have used it to catch the blood from her nose before placing it under the table.

Reed read over his report and made his final observations:

> 'I am still of the opinion that the injuries to the deceased were accidental – first, by her falling on her face, striking the bridge of her nose and fracturing it, then for a short time moved about the house with blood dripping from her and, becoming faint, fell backwards upon the enamel saucepan handles which caused the wounds and fracture to the base of the skull. I have gone into every detail of the case very carefully and have no further particulars to report.'[40]

His work done, the body buried, the family appeased, he could forget the Ridgley case and look forward to his retirement in a few months' time.

Meanwhile, Mrs Chandler and her husband found going back into 125 Nightingale Road an uncomfortable experience, particularly seeing the bloodstained items and brown paper packaging in the living room and the smears and drips of blood all over the shop. There was only one thing they could do to make the situation better, and they slowly and meticulously washed the blood from every item they could find and burned the brown packaging paper in a desperate attempt to rid themselves of the memory of this dreadful accident.

On Tuesday, 4 February, Mrs Chandler opened the shop as usual and carried on selling to the residents of Hitchin, making five pounds on the first day of business. Perhaps they could now put this dreadful matter behind them.

Chapter 11

Two Deaths Too Many

Since the end of the First World War in November 1918, Britain had been rebuilding itself, trying to find its feet. By January, following the misery of bomb-drenched London and the terrible privations that had been experienced, new signs of life were starting to appear. Hotels were full, there were queues at the best and most popular restaurants, the shops were reaping a rich harvest and the theatres were enjoying a boom. In fact, London was now more crowded than at any time in the memory of the present generation. The armistice had brought about a fresh hope, socially and politically. Political emancipation of women was back on the agenda and the machinery to enable women to vote was well under way. Herbert Asquith, the prime minister who had fallen from power during the war, losing his position to the Welshman David Lloyd George, was still emboldened enough to say that 'it is not too much to say that it [the armistice] has cleansed and purged the whole atmosphere of the world.' Sir David Brooks, the Lord Mayor of London had declared that Armistice Day was, 'the greatest day in the history of our country and it marks the beginning of a new era in human development. We must take care to use this great opportunity aright so that the world may be better and not worse by reason of the overflow of the old order.' There were high hopes for a better world, perhaps no more ably expressed than by the very British announcement that Britons were once more allowed the right to 'make cakes and pastries of every kind and to cover them with sugar or chocolate or both; and to eat an unlimited quantity of these or other cakes at afternoon tea.' But the more serious issues were also being voiced on every street corner as well as in government corridors. Three quarters of a million men had been killed in the conflict, nearly two million wounded. The 'Great War' was a war to end all wars; the Kaiser should be hanged and it must never happen again.

It wasn't long before euphoria had given way to reality and life quickly returned to the monotonous and the humdrum; the memory of police whistles being blasted on Armistice Day across the country was fast becoming a distant memory. As if there hadn't been enough death over the last four years, influenza struck at the heart of Britain in 1918 and into the first few months of 1919, claiming almost a quarter of a million civilian lives, recognising no class boundaries. It was in this context that Lloyd George went to the country to seek a mandate for domestic reform to stabilise post-war nerves, and in December he formed a cross-party government with businessmen to find the solutions.

But with gathering momentum, the problems piled up. While pre-war flour returned to the shops and street lights now blazed again, food rationing continued, particularly butter and sugar. Prices had taken a sharp, upward turn, inflation rose and many were prosecuted for food regulation violations. There was a housing shortage, probably by as many as 600,000, exacerbated by the slow return of largely discontented service personnel and the general cessation of house building throughout the war, which in turn had led to expensive rents. Lloyd George's government had won the election on a promise of building homes for returning servicemen, but it quickly became apparent that such a plan was too expensive and war heroes would simply have to go without.

On Monday, 27 January, the day Mrs Ridgley's body had been found on a bitterly cold, snowy morning, shipbuilders in Clyde called a general strike over working conditions, mainly demanding a forty-hour week. A series of walkouts followed, and four days later, the government moved in troops, tanks and machine guns. The Battle of George Street was at first a pathetic mix of struggling workers fighting with policemen armed only with truncheons and bottles of fizzy lemonade, but this was shortly followed by the Riot Act being read, police officers attacked by missiles of bottles and stones, and serious assaults and looting taking place in the city. Miners were quick to follow suit and threaten strike action, and Britain's tired troops were soon to be put to the task of controlling the very people they had recently been fighting for. Already, the government's vision of a journey to the better world felt more like a journey on an open-top bus in the depths of winter.

Matters in the police service were not good either. After leaving the army in 1911, Major Alfred Letchworth Law had been appointed Chief Constable of Hertfordshire Constabulary though he had returned to military service after the outbreak of war much to the reluctance of the standing committee, who felt that his first priority was to the role of chief constable. However, he was eventually summoned for a specific post, was promoted to lieutenant colonel and served until November 1918, when he resumed his duties as chief constable.

His appointment was a good one, having already had first-hand experience of commanding troops with the North Staffordshire Regiment in Belfast in 1898 quelling rioters and he had been the chief constable of two county forces before he was appointed to Hertfordshire. He was an ambitious man and shortly after returning from the war applied to become the commissioner of the Metropolitan Police but was unsuccessful, so now he focussed on his role of county chief constable. He carried out his duties with military precision and was renowned for his attention to detail, and he insisted that the county's policemen were, like himself, immaculately presented and highly disciplined. All his mental and physical energy was thrown at police work; intense, absolute and unremitting. He was a policeman, not a bureaucrat, and his attention to detail was extraordinary, some would say pedantic. He expected his constables to know their beats inside out and would routinely check up on them to satisfy himself they were mentally equipped to carry out their duties.

But his return hadn't been a happy one, and one on which he now brooded as he read through Reed's report. Almost immediately, he had received notice from another of his superintendents, Joseph Hassell, stating his intention to resign now that the war had ended, something which would ordinarily be quite routine. Having granted Hassell leave to retire, the superintendent had again written to Law in December 1918 asking for his retirement to be delayed due to his inability to find suitable housing, and he sought leave to remain in the police house in which he currently lived with his family. Law's opinion of Hassell was that he wasn't a 'good and efficient officer', and requiring the house for another police officer he refused to delay the matter and as a consequence Hassell had taken his own life by swallowing poison at home on 9 January. Hassell had clearly killed himself with the intent to draw criticism of the chief constable, as he had written three letters in advance which were addressed to Law, Hassell's wife and the district coroner, Lovel Smeathman, all claiming that his suicide was as a result of the chief constable's inflexibility about his delayed retirement and in effect making his family homeless. He had behaved in a 'drastically cruel and hasty manner', the letters emphasised.

The accusation had hurt Law immensely and he had been cross-examined rigorously at the inquest where he had had to admit that it was routine for retiring officers to find themselves without settled accommodation. He had, however, successfully defended himself against another accusation that he had allowed Hassell to retire due to the superintendent's recent outburst in court which had brought criticism upon himself. Hassell's letter had specifically stated that the chief constable was 'primarily to blame' for his intended suicide, an allegation which Law was finding difficult to contend with despite the inquest's verdict of 'suicide by the taking of prussic acid probably during an unsound state of mind.' Nonetheless, he recognised the plight of officers retiring from the force and that there was an acute shortage of houses for even serving officers. Consequently, he had now applied for, and been given, permission by the county council to build thirty-two policemen's cottages across the county.

Now, less than a month later, he read Reed's report with some scepticism. The superintendent's retirement was imminent and Law's reaction to the report outlining the circumstances of Mrs Ridgley's death and Reed's explanation of it was one of disbelief. He had not, Law thought, satisfactorily explained all the bloodstaining in the house, had not given a plausible reason for the extensive head injuries and had been wholly equivocal about how the grocer's dog had met its death. It played on his mind too that shopkeepers had become particularly vulnerable during the war, with much resentment being levelled at them due to food shortages and sharp increases in the cost of living, caused by the German unrestricted use of U-boats to sink food ships headed for Britain. Many had been accused of stockpiling to artificially inflate prices and it wouldn't be the first time that violence had been used against them. Not that it mattered that much, but he was also very much aware that Reed's last investigation, albeit on a much less serious matter, had resulted in the magistrates unanimously acquitting the defendant. He needed a second opinion, and he thought about the best way to achieve this without another of his superintendents reacting as dramatically as Hassell. Phrases from the dead man's letter still resonated in his ears: 'Law was a very unpopular man' it had said 'except for the few with whom he curries favour, and had acted in an ungentlemanly way.' The chief constable considered his options for a short while before arriving at his conclusion. Rather than directly challenging Reed, he would get someone else to do it. He picked up the telephone and called Scotland Yard.

Chapter 12

New Lodgings

Hertfordshire, February 1919

Annie Smith sat in the armchair in her small dining room, the county newspaper in her hand opened at the page covering Hitchin; the daily nationals rested on the table next to her. She pouted her lips as she read about poor Mrs Ridgley, who had fallen over in her shop and killed herself; not that she could fully understand how her dog had been killed as well. She knew the grocer, and as the shop was only a couple of hundred yards away she went there several times each week to get the things she needed for the house. It would all be different now. No one to chat to about the weather, the gossip. What would become of the shop, she thought, as she looked up from the paper, suddenly realising the impact of the loss of a neighbour. She remembered the evening that Mrs Ridgley had met her death, though. It was the night her new lodger, John Healy, had been seen hanging around outside the grocer's shop by her daughter, Mavis. She even remembered her coming in and mentioning it to Healy's wife, Annie, who seemed to be somewhat embarrassed about her husband not being at home. Mavis had been quick to sense her awkwardness and quickly changed the subject; she was a sensible girl like that.

She didn't have much time for Healy. Since he and his wife had arrived at the lodging house in Radcliffe Road just before Christmas, he had developed into a bit of a drunk, and violent with it, often shouting at and, she suspected, beating his wife when no one else was about. She hoped they would find new lodgings soon. He had already fallen behind with his rent, although surprisingly he had recently paid off his outstanding debt – a few days after Mrs Ridgley's body had been found, in fact. He had received his army war gratuity payment apparently, which had stopped the landlady from having to ask them to leave. She glanced at the clock in her living room, which was always half an hour fast, moved her attention back to the newspaper and, having finished reading the short article about the tragic accident, she looked for other Hitchin news.

Chapter 13

The Yard Arrives

Hertfordshire, Thursday, 6 February 1919

Detective Chief Inspector Wensley sat quietly in the railway carriage as it rattled along on its journey from London to Hitchin and glanced down casually at the file he had been handed from his boss in Scotland Yard. The request from the Chief Constable of Hertfordshire Constabulary written on the front cover gave little by way of clues: 'Ask that a CID officer be sent to assist in making enquiries respecting the murder of Mrs Ridgley at Hitchin between the 25th and 27th January last. Would like to see the officer at Hatfield as soon as possible,' it read. He stared back out of the window, briefly glancing at the four police officers he had brought to help him: Detective Sergeant George Brewer, whose shorthand skills when interviewing witnesses had proven invaluable in the past; his colleague Detective Sergeant Cooper; Detective Constable William Waters, a brilliant plan drawer; and Detective Sergeant William McBride, the Yard's first official photographer. Knowing he had brought a good team with him, though, didn't hide his concern about being called in so late to investigate the matter. Ten days had now passed since the woman's body had been found, and he gritted his teeth and gently shook his head wondering what he would soon be presented with.

Arriving at the police headquarters in Hatfield, they were ushered into the chief constable's office, Alfred Law looking Wensley up and down as if making his first impressions of the Scotland Yard senior detective. Wensley carefully removed his below-knee-length wool overcoat and bowler hat and hung them on the coat rack in the corner of the office, together with his snow-laden umbrella. His colleagues did the same. Wensley's immaculate suit and shiny shoes must have caught the eye of the chief constable; he had every intention of impressing upon him that he been given the best man for the job. The Chief Constable started to talk.

The Metropolitan detectives sat and listened to the ex-military man summarise his superintendent's report in serious mood. Sitting next to him was his Chief Clerk, Superintendent George Knight, who was responsible for disciplinary matters within the constabulary. Reed, said the chief constable, had concluded that death was due to accidental causes, the dog had been killed by the deceased, and that there was, overall, an absence of motive for murder. His instructions were clear; he wanted an independent investigation before he could accept that view.[41] He handed Reed's reports to Wensley and apologised for not having called Scotland Yard earlier, and then he ended the meeting by stating that the matter should be 'strictly investigated and satisfactorily cleared up.'

Wensley took his brief from the chief constable and was quietly pleased with the man in charge of the force. Much criticism had been levelled at retired army officers for the dictatorial manner in which they'd assumed their new positions in rural forces, but this was a time when strong leadership was necessary, and Law looked like he would provide it.

Despite his wealth of experience and his successful record in murder investigations, which had been rewarded with numerous commendations, Wensley knew that the small town of Hitchin presented a significant challenge, and one made more difficult by the unfriendly reception he received from George Reed, aggrieved that someone was challenging his judgement. Reed went with Wensley and Sergeant Brewer to the shop at Nightingale Road, where they met PC Kirby and Mary Chandler, who was slightly confused about the arrival of different police officers – hadn't this all been cleared up?

The detective chief inspector informed Mrs Chandler that the chief constable had asked him to review the investigation and asked whether it would be possible for him to have access to the premises for a short period while he carried out his own enquiries. The woman from London was in many ways relieved to have the opportunity to go back home and get away from the house in which she still remained uncomfortable, and she willingly handed over the keys to the detective. Wensley had already been told what Chandler had told the local police but wanted to speak to her in greater detail before she went back to the capital.

She went over again how her sister had other siblings; George, William and Henry Gordon and sisters Annie Wilson, Ellen Eades and Emily Pollard. Elizabeth herself had been widowed in 1917 and that she had an estranged stepson, with whom she wasn't on good terms and hadn't seen since his father's death just before Christmas. She described her sister's routine of opening and closing the shop and told him that, while the dog was friendly towards customers, the Irish terrier would never allow anyone to walk into the private part of the house. Her money was also dealt with in a routine of counting it each day and entering the details into a book, but despite not having a bank account, she would never keep more than a week's takings on the premises, spending the rest on buying new stock. On Saturdays, typically, she would take the day's takings upstairs, usually about £10, count it and then enter the details the following day.

Wensley had already been made aware that Ridgley would typically take about £23 a week over the counter and he knew that in many people's eyes, this made her a wealthy woman.

The cigar box and treacle tin which had been found in the passageway were used for holding cash in the till drawer, and she kept all her counted money in a box behind the living room door. No one, she said, had any grievances against her sister, whom she had last seen when she came to London to buy some stock four days before her body was found.[42] Confused about something written in Reed's report, Wensley asked her about the broom, which was apparently resting against the armchair in the living room, not somewhere he expected it to be. The sister confirmed his suspicions, telling him that it was always kept in the scullery. He thanked her for the additional information and Mrs Chandler left for London.

Reed, now agitated and annoyed that he had been kept waiting, gruffly told Wensley that Constable Kirby would show him around the house and suggested that they use the front upstairs room of the house as a base from which they could operate. He had presumed that Wensley would only be in town for a couple of days at most and made his way back to the police station.

Even though Mrs Ridgley's sister had been at the shop for four days, inside remained bitterly cold. The snow had settled outside and the small fire in the living room gave off little heat, creating a very unwelcoming and inhospitable environment.

In some ways, working from the house was better for Wensley as he saw the majority of his enquiries being carried out either at the premises or speaking to neighbours, but nonetheless this was going to be a largely unpleasant task. Kirby, sensing the unease and seemingly not a little embarrassed about the investigation so far, suggested to Wensley that he showed him around the house, for which Wensley, with a modicum of a smile, thanked him. The local constable gave the entire story, from entering the house and finding the body, where he had seen blood and, importantly, where he had found the weight, cigar box and the various amounts of cash around the premises. As they walked through the house, Wensley and Brewer listened carefully and sensed that Constable Alf Kirby was keen to show that the Hertfordshire Constabulary was an able and competent force, and they were privately pleased that he had been assigned by Reed to assist the Metropolitan detectives in any way he could.

After they'd satisfied themselves that they had a full understanding of the scene, they huddled together in the front upstairs room discussing the statements taken from the immediate neighbours and the additional information that had just been gleaned from the deceased's sister. Wensley made his first decision. Reed and Kirby were to rearrange everything in the shop, as far as they were able, so that it was exactly the way it was when Kirby first entered the premises on 27 January and found the bloodstained body.[43] The need to preserve any fingerprint evidence was paramount; but the pots, kettles, broom handles, counter and, most importantly, the cigar box, cardboard receptacle and four-pound weight needed to be put back in exactly the same place. Using Reed would ensure there would be no suggestion that Kirby had made any mistakes or that his memory had failed him.

The following morning, the local constable, with the less than happy Superintendent George Reed breathing over his shoulder, mustered his memory and carefully rearranged everything until he was certain that everything was as he had found it. Reed nodded agreement. McBride and Waters, two of the officers who had accompanied Wensley, took a series of photographs on the inside of the premises and drew a detailed scaled plan.[44] The scene was now as controlled as it was going to be, but it was a pity, brooded Wensley, that the body had been removed. Never mind. At least he had the weight and the two blood-smeared boxes from the till drawer, which could reveal some interesting fingerprints. Fingerprint evidence was now well established in the courts, and science had moved on at an amazing speed since he had joined the service in 1888. It was now accepted that everyone had a unique fingerprint, and he recalled the first case in which fingerprint evidence secured a conviction for Alfred and Albert Stratton, who, in March 1905 broke into a shop in Deptford High Street, killing the manager and his wife. They were hanged in May of the same year at Wandsworth, their infamy assured because of the ground-breaking evidence that sent them to the gallows. This would probably be his best chance to rescue something from this disaster, and he arranged for the items to be more closely examined.

He now wasted no time. He wanted to personally speak to the three witnesses who had already provided information about the finding of the body and when she was last seen. He summoned Inspectors Warren and Bowyer to go over events again and was wholly unimpressed with Warren, who showed remarkable indifference about what he had seen. Warren's language was evasive, as he played down the amount of blood and the nature of the wounds found on Mrs Ridgley's body and Wensley formed the impression that either he was a complete incompetent or he was seeking to protect Reed, his superintendent.[45] He was equally dismayed with the paucity of information that had been committed to paper, some of which remained unsigned and undated, and he spoke to each of the witnesses, asking them to tell their stories again. Annie Withey repeated her discussion with the shopkeeper at about 8.20pm on the Saturday evening and could only add that a number of people were returning home from the cinema at that time and they may be able to help.[46] Frank Wheeler, who had accompanied Kirby into the house, merely confirmed everything that the constable had said about the finding of the body,[47] but Mrs Roach and her seventeen-year-old son were able to paint a more detailed picture of the events of Saturday evening.

Their house at 126, Nightingale Road abutted the grocer shop, and so it was a frequent occurrence to hear noises from the next-door neighbour. Louisa Roach wasn't on particularly good terms with Mrs Ridgley over some minor disagreement, which may explain her inaction, as she had described to PC Kirby a week or so ago. She heard, she now said, the sounds of her neighbour closing the shop, although not the bolting of the front door, and at some stage after about 8.15pm, she heard the unusual sound of the dog barking followed by a couple of thuds. She jokingly said to her children, 'Oh, she is killing the dog,' to which her son Leslie had replied, 'You do think some funny things, Mother. I expect she is chopping his head off.' Wensley found this information to be most interesting and probed the son further. He remembered that he had listened to the noises, *four* distinct thuds, he recalled, and thought perhaps a child was next door and had said, 'They have got a baby in there. It is crying.'[48]

So, soon into his investigation, Wensley knew he had stumbled across something. If Reed had known this at the time, if he had bothered to properly investigate, would he have been quite so happy to conclude that this was an accident? The thuds, the crying, all began to paint a different picture. Louisa reiterated what she had already told Warren and Kirby, that some time between midnight and 2am she heard the sound of moaning but had dismissed it as a noise coming from number 124. She had looked out of the window, seen two people walking past, and had gone back to bed, although, to Wensley's amazement, stayed awake until the moaning had stopped. Had she been on more friendly terms with Ridgley, she may, just may, have investigated further. But she hadn't. It would be a further thirty-two hours before her immediate next-door neighbour's body would be found. Wensley now made his second big decision. With no body to examine and with a complicated cleaned-up bloodstained scene to interpret, he decided to contact someone who would help to move the investigation along; Bernard Spilsbury.

Spilsbury had been appointed Home Office pathologist in 1910. After a mediocre academic background, he had trained as a doctor, developed an acute interest in pathology, and had quickly shown great promise. His elevation to his current position had largely been secured as a result of his analysis and the evidence he had had given in the Crippen trial in 1910 and had received further notoriety five years later through his explanation at court of the deaths of a number of George Joseph Smith's wives, who had allegedly died as a result of fits while in their baths. In both cases, it was largely Spilsbury's evidence that had led to murder convictions and had sent both of them to the gallows. By 1918, his reputation was such that, as soon as he attended a post mortem examination, people would say that the accused was as good as convicted and sentenced to death. His mere presence in court was powerful ammunition for the Crown. Such was his self-confidence that he denied being infallible but had said, 'I have never claimed to be God, but merely His locum on His days off.'

He prided himself on his medical achievements and his ability to interpret injuries to corpses, but he was also fastidious about his appearance, his six foot two frame sporting immaculate suits and his trademark spats. It wasn't unknown for him to sport a flower in his buttonhole when giving evidence in court, though somewhat incongruous to this outward appearance of sartorial elegance was his habit of smoking fifty cigarettes a day. His boldness in appearance was matched by his staunch views on controversial matters and he didn't hide his belief in capital punishment.

Wensley's investigations had brought him into contact with Spilsbury many times before, and just a few hours after being contacted, the two were reunited in Hitchin. The pathologist looked around the house and was shown the weight and the clothes and handkerchief which had been removed from the body. Frustrated by his inability to see the body, he asked if he could at least see the carcase of the dog. Goldsmith was urgently contacted, who, to the delight of the two men, announced that although Reed had told him to dispose of it, he had chosen to keep the dog at his surgery. He, too, hadn't been convinced of the outcome of the earlier police investigation. Three days later, Spilsbury examined the Irish terrier, hoping to find evidence of clothing in its teeth, but he found nothing. However, cutting into the scalp and pulling back the skin across the top of the head, he exposed a fracture on the left-hand side of the skull. Goldsmith looked embarrassed and closed his eyes as he rued his decision not to examine the dog more carefully the week before. But Spilsbury was far too immersed inside the skull of the Irish terrier to notice, and he quickly came to the conclusion that Reed's assumption about the cause of death wasn't consistent with the injuries. If he had got that wrong, the next step was obvious.

The pathologist recommended to Wensley that despite any embarrassment which may arise, application should be made to the coroner for Mrs Ridgley's body to be exhumed. Without the opportunity to examine the body in detail, any further investigation would be seriously constrained. Such a move would undoubtedly open up the Hertfordshire Constabulary wounds to a large dose of salt, and Wensley considered the ramifications as Spilsbury made his way back to London. But he also recalled the Chief Constable of Hertfordshire's direction in this matter; he required that the matter be 'strictly investigated and satisfactorily cleared up'. He picked up the telephone and spoke to the coroner.

Chapter 14

A Picture Emerges

The news was now starting to spread around the town that the Metropolitan Police had been called in to reinvestigate the accidental death of Mrs Ridgley. Until this point, local newspapers had reported how the grocer had fallen over and somehow killed herself. Wensley frowned awkwardly as he read the latest edition of the *Bedfordshire Express* published on Saturday, 8 February, two days after he had arrived in Hitchin, based on the Hertfordshire Constabulary's investigation, but, as far as the reading public would be concerned, this would be what Wensley himself was thinking. Nothing could be further from the truth. He read the report again, cursing. 'There is still no explanation of the death of Mrs Ridgley', it said, 'and none is expected even after the adjourned inquest date of 19 February'. It continued. 'On 19 February, the local police surgeon, Dr Grellett, is expected to give evidence of his post mortem and the police will provide results of the further examination of the scene'. Wensley physically shook as he read the next line. 'Trade has continued at the shop despite the grim shadow which hovers over the house.' Not any longer, he thought, before continuing to read what Superintendent Reed had previously released to the newspapers. He, Reed, had actually been quoted as saying that a number of khaki handkerchiefs have been found in the shop for sale, *thus eliminating the source of the handkerchief around her neck.* What's more, a local police sergeant's wife had apparently seen her using one of them, although the sergeant, but not the newspapers, had subsequently been told that she may have been mistaken.[49] 'The police are convinced,' said the journalists, 'that all the injuries to the head could have been caused by the woman falling on the pile of crockery and the sharp, enamelled handles, resulting in blood being found all over them.' What *is* this, thought Wensley, a Hitchin conspiracy to avoid an admission of murder? The newspaper article also put into the public domain details which Wensley would have preferred to have kept back for now; that the four-pound weight had normally been used for weighing vegetables, how much money had been found in the house, the fact that blood had been found on the bolt of the front door, burnt matches had been found inside the premises, and that the dog had died as a result of one blow to the head which the vet, Goldsmith, had described as 'a lucky shot'. At least the national newspapers were still heading their articles using the word 'murder' and how the local police are baffled, but he wondered just how many of the Hitchin residents read them.

His frustration intensified as he thought about the unprofessional manner of Reed's investigation. If it had been a minor matter investigated to this standard by one of his constables, he would have disciplined him for sure. The standards expected had been recently circulated nationwide in police circles and much emphasis had been placed on the police gathering evidence meticulously. He remembered the circulation:

> 'The first principle to be laid down on this subject is that the strictest accuracy is to be observed in giving evidence as it is of the highest importance for the administration of justice that the evidence of the Police should be unimpeachable. For this purpose, the habit of careful and accurate observation should be cultivated in regard to all matters relating to the work of the Police. Written notes of the particulars of any case are to be made at the time in order that the Constable may be able to refresh his memory in regard to details if called on to give evidence. If more than one Constable is engaged on a case the rule should be that these notes should not be compared or discussed, in order that evidence in each case may be quite independent.'

These rules applied equally to an offence of vagrancy as they did to one of murder, and Reed's blinkered approach coupled with the minimalist attitude towards identifying witnesses and information fell far short of the standards outlined. No wonder police forces up and down the country were crying out for detective training.

All these incompetent aspects of the investigation caused him a moment of embarrassment; not for himself but for the police service as a whole. It was only a few months earlier, in August 1918, that the police had walked out on strike demanding better pay and better working conditions and now they had achieved most of what they had asked for, here they were trying to convince the very people they were meant to be working for, the public, that poor Mrs Ridgley had met her end by accident when quite clearly, she had been bludgeoned to death.

He dwelt on the details of the strike, shuddering as he remembered the pain and awkwardness it had caused when five thousand police officers from all over London – out of a total of 19,000 – had descended upon 10, Downing Street, bringing the capital to a standstill at a time when so many men were still being slaughtered in the trenches of Flanders. Had they no sense of patriotism and duty? He understood the men's plight. He knew only too well from his own experience that pay was poor, working conditions were awful and families of those who had gone on strike were barely able to feed themselves, but their timing had been misjudged. The men had turned up in the heart of a war-weary government waving the banners of the National Union of Police and Prison Officers, a body decreed illegal by the then commissioner, Sir Edward Henry, who had openly declared that any officer or constable who joined the union would be instantly dismissed. Wensley recalled stories of Winston Churchill having to fight his way through the crowd of officers in plain clothes, and soldiers who had been swiftly brought in to maintain some sort of order, to get to the entrance of Downing Street the very man who in 1910 had approved the reduction of the police working week to six days. Now, as a member of the War Cabinet, he had been summoned to the Cabinet Room by the prime minister, Lloyd George, to help negotiate some sort of resolution. Such was the depth of feeling within the police union, who had considered the government to have been rather dilatory in their willingness to consider a much-needed pay rise, and were dismissive of the union's allegations of bullying and corruption, that they felt they genuinely had no alternative but to call a strike, putting the very fabric of British society at risk. But this was a time of war and general civil unrest and it had made people very nervous.

Lloyd George now presided over a crisis of great magnitude and was confronted by deep, contrasting opinion. 'The strikers are men mutinying in the face of the enemy,' Sir Frederick Wodehouse, the assistant commissioner of police had said. 'They have laid the capital open to sabotage and other grave dangers.' Others, like Sir Edward Henry had apparently physically shivered as he remembered a lunatic trying to shoot him six years earlier and couldn't contemplate a society without a police force. But his position had looked increasingly untenable, a man Lloyd George considered to have been wholly responsible for not having seen the looming disaster. The Home Secretary, Sir George Cave, had been indifferent and hadn't helped with his attitude in recent times towards police pay and was without doubt a significant factor in poor police morale. Lloyd George had sat and listened to representatives of the police union, his mind made even more focussed by the noise of the crowd outside his front door and occupying most of Whitehall, the very streets where, just before the war, the police had fought with suffragettes over the right of women to vote.

The prime minister, though, had moved swiftly. His ministers and senior police staff had let him down, but he had been desperate to ensure that unionism wasn't allowed to spread into the police force. The next thing would be a unionised military, the tail wagging the dog, and all discipline and control would be lost. This, in the middle of one of the bloodiest and probably most enduring of world crises. He had instructed that the issue of police pay be immediately addressed and had given assurances that all the other issues raised by the unofficial union would be dealt with. Within a short time, pay and pensions were increased and war bonuses were granted. However, he had stood firm on the issue of recognition of the police union and stated unequivocally that no such body could exist that would diminish the commissioner's control of discipline. A union which could call the men out on strike was fundamentally wrong, he had argued, but had given an undertaking that once the war had finished, hopefully by the summer of 1919, consideration would be given to a body of representatives that could speak for the constables and officers of the Metropolitan Police. The officers who had been put forward to negotiate with the government had accepted this offer and within forty-five hours of the strike being called, constables had returned to their beats.

Gasps of relief within Whitehall were palpable, and Lloyd George had returned to the rather more important issue of winning the war, but not before he had made one final decision. Never before had the streets of government been so ruthlessly invaded. Never before had the country been so close to Bolshevism. Newspapers had even dared to suggest that the strike was instigated by the Kaiser himself, designed to undermine that most British institution, the police service. It was intolerable. He required Sir Edward Henry to resign and replaced him with Sir Nevil Macready, the only man whom he considered suitable to continue to deal with police grievances and turn the force into an efficient body of men. If they existed, bribery, corruption, perjury and bullying needed to become things of the past.

Something good had come of the strike, thought Wensley. He liked Macready. He would be good for the force. He had the same work ethic as himself and he had quickly recognised the weaknesses of the superintending ranks in the Metropolitan Police. He wondered what he would have made of Reed.

He put down the newspaper, stared out of the window from the cold, smelly, damp upstairs room in Nightingale Road and, twisting one end of his neatly-groomed moustache, tried to gather his thoughts and forget what had gone before. He and his team had started to build a picture of the last-known movements of the deceased, including a statement from Ernest Mansell, a ten-year-old boy who had been in the shop with his mother at 7.30pm on the Saturday and had been sent out to fetch Ridgley a pint of beer from the nearby Woolpack Inn in Starling's Place. This accounted for the beer on the living room table found by Kirby. Also, eleven-year-old Arthur Massey said he had gone into the shop just after 8pm with a friend of his and he saw a man there wearing a hard hat with a dark overcoat and wearing a collar and tie. He had pimples on his face, and Mrs Ridgley was wearing a blue apron, the eleven-year-old exclaimed, pleased with his powers of recollection.[50]

He had also been very interested in a particular witness who had presented himself at the front door of the shop, offering information. William Augustus Craswell, a thirty-two-year-old tailor, had asked to speak to whoever was in charge. He had been welcomed in and he had quietly told the officers that he had known Mrs Ridgley and had been in her shop at 8.20pm on Saturday, 25 January, had bought some bread and had stood there for a while chatting away to her. While talking to her, two men had come in. The first, who he had recognised as a regular customer but didn't know his name, bought some tobacco and matches, which the shopkeeper kept under the counter, and left; at some point the dog had actually jumped up onto the counter and was quickly pushed off by its owner. Then another man had appeared at the shop doorway. He had obviously entered by the front door but had paused at the hallway entrance and looked inside. He had asked Mrs Ridgley for something – he couldn't remember what – was told that she didn't have it and he turned and left the premises.[51] Shortly afterwards, Craswell had said goodnight to Mrs Ridgley and left. At that time, there was no one in there.

His story had been interesting but was something that had happened ten minutes before Annie Withey had exchanged words with the deceased but at least it went to confirm that Mrs Ridgley was alive and well around this time. It was also clear that Craswell was likely to be the 'pimple-faced' man with the hard hat seen in the shop by Mansell. Slowly, Wensley was identifying and eliminating people from his enquiry, but who was the man who had bought the tobacco and matches? At last he had some sort of lead, and this man would become the focus of his investigation.

Over the following days, statements were taken from Gertrude Day and Edwin Sutton about the discovery of the body – none had been taken to date – and further information was obtained about Mrs Ridgley's estranged stepson, William, who had now been located. One of the deceased's few friends in Hitchin, and only regular visitor outside of the family, Kate Gilbert, confirmed to the police that the shopkeeper wasn't on friendly terms with the stepson and on the rare occasions he visited she always asked her to be present in the house although no reason for this apparent dislike was ever given.[52] Enquiries quickly revealed that the stepson had in fact attended the funeral, and it appeared as though it was nothing more than a dislike of each other. Simply, he didn't like his father's new wife. The stepson was eliminated.

By 12 February, Sergeant Brewer had interviewed John Chandler, the brother-in-law of the dead woman, and had established the grocer's pattern of behaviour in her running of the business and how she lived her life. He was able to clarify the layout of the house, pointing out that the dog would sleep in the basket in the living room during the day and would be kept out of the shop area by placing the wooden planks, found by Kirby, across the entrance to the hallway. He confirmed the four-pound weight was normally kept by the scales in the kitchen/scullery area and was used for weighing potatoes. As soon as it got dark, she always bolted the back door and lit a candle in the living room as well as lighting the paraffin lamp hanging above the shop counter. At the same time, she always brought her stock in from outside and pulled down the blind on the front door, a practice she had continued since the war when complying with the Lighting Order but now used to stop children from leaning against her door and peering in.[53] At closing time, she always bolted the front door and emptied the till. She had an established routine of removing the cash from the till drawer behind the counter, putting the money into her pocket, extinguishing the lamp and going into the living room for her supper before retiring to bed. He was unable to say how and when she entered the details in the memorandum book, but he offered something which was an exciting development. When asked by Brewer whether she ever used or wore khaki handkerchiefs, he said she didn't, and when shown the now ink-stained as well as bloodstained handkerchief that had been removed from the body, he was emphatic that it wasn't hers and was unable to identify it.

From all the evidence Wensley had now managed to gather, he was convinced that at some time after 8.30pm on Saturday, 25 January, someone had entered the shop and violently murdered Mrs Ridgley using the four-pound weight, gagging the woman's cries by smothering her with his own khaki handkerchief. Presuming the dog to have reacted to his owner being attacked, he thought that it too was bludgeoned to death with the same weapon. Having beaten them both to death, the attacker locked the front door to ensure he wasn't disturbed, thus accounting for the blood on the bolt. As to why, he was sure it was for money. Even though much cash had been found on the premises, there was none that appeared to be the apparent takings for Saturday. Only a few pennies were found on her body when searched at the mortuary and a few farthings were in the till. As to who, he had no idea, but he was convinced that if he continued to ask the right questions of the right people he would soon find out. Someone had desperately needed money and wasn't far away. With the bit between his teeth, Wensley left the shop and headed to see the coroner.

He was about to cause a stir.

Chapter 15

The New Theory

Francis Shillitoe, the coroner, didn't need much convincing. On 13 February, he issued a warrant ordering the exhumation of Elizabeth Ridgley.[54] Its wording reinforced the gravity of the situation:

> 'Whereas I, Francis Shillitoe, Coroner for the Hitchin district of the County of Hertford have been requested by the Home Office Pathologist to produce to him the body of a woman named Elizabeth Ridgley which has been buried by my order in the Burial Ground in the Parish of Hitchin in the said County. These are therefore in His Majesty's name and by virtue of my office to charge and command you that you forthwith cause the body of the said Elizabeth Ridgley to be taken up that I may proceed with my inquest. Herewith fail not as you will answer the contrary at your peril.
>
> 'Given under my hand and seal this 13th day of February, 1919.
>
> (Signed) Francis Shillitoe
> Coroner for the Hitchin District of the said County.'

Two days later, George Kirby, the undertaker who had buried her only two weeks earlier, removed the coffin from Hitchin cemetery and conveyed it to the mortuary, identifying its contents to Dr Spilsbury. Dr Grellett, who had examined her just over a fortnight ago, stood by his side; so too did Wensley.

Grellett's opinion of the cause of death hadn't changed, and he was pleased about this extraordinary turn of events and that a forensic pathologist was conducting a second examination. He had read in the newspaper about the police theory that Mrs Ridgley had met her death through an accident and was astounded. He had intended to repeat his theory about the cause of death when he was due to give evidence at the inquest on 19 February, but now that the matter was being reinvestigated, he was much relieved.

The forensic pathologist got to work, and after making a few notes about her height of five foot four and that she was sparsely built, he methodically examined the body, focussing extensively on the injuries to the head. He noted four lacerations to the back of the skull towards the right ear, all of which were bruised, and one so open that a fracture beneath it could be seen. Lesser cuts were obvious on the left eye and lower lip as well as a number of bruises on both arms and across the right shoulder, which were in all probability caused as she used her arms to defend herself against attack. The lower left jaw was fractured and two other fractures appeared at the base of the skull. His findings were much more comprehensive than that of Grellett's earlier, rather cursory examination, and he was prepared to offer an opinion. The cause of death, he announced assertively to Wensley, was due to meningeal haemorrhage of the brain caused by the fractures, but which were inflicted 'at the same time and by the same implement'. Unconsciousness would have been induced almost immediately and the injuries 'must have been inflicted by someone and not caused by falling'. The four-pound weight, which Spilsbury had now examined, or a poker, could have caused the injuries; certainly, a blunt instrument had been used. He went further. Considerable force must have been used to inflict the injuries, and due to the thickness of the skin and hair at the point of fracture, the injuries were sustained while the woman was lying face down on the floor. By inspecting the marks beneath the wounds, he was certain that each of the four lacerations to the head had been inflicted from different directions. However, the bruises close to the right ear were caused by a single blow and the general bruising to the head was caused by the woman being dragged on the floor by the hair while she was still alive, thus the unusual final resting position of her heels pointing upwards and her toes facing towards the floor. Finally, because he had examined the whole of Mrs Ridgley's body, he noted the presence of blood in the intestine, which suggested that the deceased survived the attack for some time, although in all probability she would have been unconscious.

Grellett and Wensley raised eyebrows at each other; Grellett through relief as much as anything else, Wensley through satisfaction that his call to the coroner had been vindicated.

With the results of the post mortem resonating in their thoughts, the pathologist and detective returned to the shop to re-examine the ground floor. Spilsbury was clear; Mrs Ridgley received the majority of her injuries in the passageway, although one at least, judging by the blood spattering on the glass cabinet being 4 feet 9 inches above the floor, was inflicted in the living room. The dog, had at various points, taken a series of blows to the head with a blunt instrument.[55]

It was now the detective's turn. He too was clear. He had never accepted Reed's theory about the deceased falling and then stumbling around the property. Had she done so, blood would have been on the bottom of her shoes and there had been none. Similarly, judging by the blood-saturated clothes removed from her body, had she been crawling or stumbling around, heavy smearing of blood would have been present on the floor. None of the police officers nor the Chandlers had said they'd seen anything consistent with this. And why would she kill her dog, one she was very fond of and was doubtlessly there to offer some sort of protection? If she had used the handkerchief to stem the flow of blood from her wounds as Reed concluded, why would she bother to wrap it around her neck and tie it at the back? No, someone, probably a man, judging by the level of violence used, entered the shop through the front door shortly after Annie Withey spoke to Ridgley at 8.30pm and somehow caused her to go to the living room, probably by asking for something that she kept there. Once she was out of the shop, he tried to steal from the till by reaching over the counter but was unable to open the drawer due to a catch which prevented it from opening. Frustrated, he walked through to the passageway, where he was confronted by the shopkeeper and her dog. This, in his opinion, accounted for the neighbour hearing the dog bark, and the noises she heard were caused by the intruder picking up the weight, which was close to the hallway door leading into the kitchen, and attacking the woman and her dog close to the living room, where most of the blood had been found. In all probability, the dog attacked the intruder as it attempted to protect its owner and, more than likely, resulted in the attacker being quite badly injured. Repeated blows to the victims while their bodies were held on the floor would account for the 'thuds' heard by the Roach family and, having stunned or killed his victims, he went back to the front door, bolted it, and then successfully opened the till from behind the counter, leaving both either smeared or dripped in blood. Aided by the light from matches he had lit from the dozens of packets in the shop, he stole the contents of the till, the Saturday takings, and then left through the back door, disappearing into the cold, dark night. Once more reflecting on how things may have been different had the Roach family next door been more curious, he felt they'd displayed 'a regrettable indifference amounting to callousness'.

It was now 15 February, nineteen days since Mrs Ridgley's body had been found. Dr Spilsbury returned to London to compile his report, and it was time for the Metropolitan detective to tell the newspapers a different story.

He needed to find the man in the shop who had bought the tobacco and matches.

Chapter 16

An Arrest

Wensley had been most put out by earlier reporting of the matter in the newspapers but recognised that it had been brought about by woeful policing and a fixed and incorrect view about the cause of death. By 15 February, he had briefed journalists on what he felt confident and safe to release and they relished it with gusto. Under the title of 'The Hitchin Mystery – Scotland Yard called in', on 15 February the *Hertfordshire Express* described how the police had reconstructed the scene of the 'supposed crime' and were keen to take evidence from anyone on the following points:

> 'Strange man or men seen near Nightingale Road on the evening of Saturday, January 25;
> Any man with bloodstained clothing seen in or near Hitchin;
> Anyone attempting to cash bloodstained Treasury notes;
> Any man who wanted his forearm or hand – probably the left– dressed.'

Wensley's points on which he now invited witnesses to come forward largely came from the evidence of William Craswell and his own and Spilsbury's interpretation of the scene. He wanted to give the public something they could talk about in the hope that someone, somewhere, would say something. Having now satisfied himself on the cause of death and with Spilsbury's assistance in interpreting the scene, he wanted to announce more forcefully that this was now a murder investigation. Scanning the other newspapers, he had surrounded himself with, he read that a large fire in Hitchin had almost killed fifty-nine prisoners of war still being held captive, but all had been lucky enough to escape. It was this attention to local news that worried him, knowing that the residents were likely to be more interested in something as dramatic as a large fire rather than the police publicly declaring they had made a mistake.

But he needn't have concerned himself too much over his delayed announcement, for he now received a letter,[56] which he knew immediately was what he had been waiting for. He read it again. It said that a man named John Healy, a tall labourer, was living at 16, Radcliffe Road and had been seen loitering about outside the deceased's premises between 8.20pm and 8.30pm on 25 January. He had returned home much later than usual, about 10.30pm, and contrary to his custom went straight to bed. The following morning, Sunday, 26 January, he had the index finger of his right hand bandaged, and since the accidental death theory had been exploded, he seldom went out of an evening.

He lost not a moment. Brewer, who had been sitting opposite him, had the letter put under his nose accompanied by an instruction to find Kirby and Waters, call a taxi and prepare themselves for an arrest. Looking at a map of Hitchin, he realised that Radcliffe Road was in walking distance of where he was sitting, and the story became even more believable. Could it be that the murderer had been sitting on his guilt only a few hundred yards from where he had been working for the past week? His thoughts were disturbed as Kirby shouted from downstairs that the taxi had arrived. He put on his bowler hat and overcoat and went to make his move.

Wensley gathered his thoughts as the taxi they had summoned made its way the few hundred yards to Radcliffe Road. He thought about Mrs Ridgley and how vulnerable she must have been. There was a great deal of money and food all under one roof; no wonder she needed a dog to protect herself. He had already calculated that a man on foot could walk from the shop in Nightingale Road along Garden Row to 16 Radcliffe Road in under a minute. Everything the letter had said pointed to more than just another piece of information.

Without moving his head and through a subtle adjustment of his eyes he glanced briefly at Alf Kirby, the constable who had been directed to accept that Mrs Ridgley's death was an accident but who had proven to be an enthusiastic officer and who must be privately rejoicing that the police now had a positive lead. Wensley had grown to like him; he was hard-working and keen to learn. Wensley had taken the time to sit down with him and explain how matters may have been done differently and should another unexplained death come his way, it was far better to move and touch nothing before photographs had been taken. That way, there could be no dispute about what was where. He had impressed upon him that the role of the doctor was to certify death and no more, and he had no authority to move the body until photographs had been taken.

Moreover, the fingerprints of the deceased should always be taken so that they could be compared to any found at the scene and eliminated as potential marks of a murderer.[57] Kirby had appreciated the on-the-job training and was keen to learn more.

Even though the journey was short, Wensley considered what he was just about to go and do. He had established that the house accommodated mainly Irish 'members of the artisan class'[58] and it was likely that he wasn't going to get a warm reception. Calculating that violence was likely and knowing that finding bloodstained clothing and money was paramount, he instructed the policemen to make sure there were no fights or anything which would draw blood from Healy. He didn't want him bleeding all over the place and destroying vital clues.[59] To ensure that their visit was a surprise, he even instructed Kirby to put on some plain clothes; he didn't want the sight of a uniform to frustrate his attempt to arrest this man.

But even deeper thoughts were at play. His outward professionalism and seemingly natural aptitude to policing belied an undercurrent of personal tragedy, of which he rarely spoke.

He was a married man and had three children, two of which, Frederick and Harold, joined the army at the outbreak of the First World War. Both were identified as very capable officers and their military futures were promising, but in August 1916, Frederick, then a lieutenant in the Lincolnshire Regiment, was killed by a shell in the trenches. Two years later, Harold died of bronchial pneumonia within four days of the armistice in November 1918, only three months ago. He had built shrines to both of them in his house in Palmer's Green, displaying their photographs, war medals and details of their military records, which he intended would remain there until the day he himself died. In truth, he had not got over their deaths. Yet, despite this, after the war, not only did he calmly and methodically progress in his career, he was also involved in occasional secret, dangerous work in Ireland, counteracting anti-British activities in the build-up to the political and military arguments over Irish Home Rule. He never spoke of this work and only once hinted at anything which would suggest that this type of work was life-threatening, leaving a parcel with one of his colleagues just before he travelled across to Ireland, asking him to deliver it to his wife, Laura, known to almost everyone as Lottie, if he didn't return. Now, in peacetime Britain, he prepared to confront an Irishman, a violent Irishman probably, and he wasn't at all sure how the man would respond to an English policeman accusing him of murder.

He told the driver to pull up just short; he didn't want to alert anyone he was coming. Walking the last hundred yards in silence, they arrived at

8.30pm and knocked on the front door. They were let in by Annie Smith, the landlady, but were immediately confronted by a woman with a broad southern Irish accent demanding to know who they were. The language was choice.

On being told that they were the police and they wished to speak to a man called John Healy, she erupted into a tirade of abuse. It was clear she was Mrs Healy, and recognising that the commotion would alert her husband, he asked the landlady where the man was and was directed to the rear first-floor bedroom. Moving faster than the ranting Irish woman, he darted up the stairs, Brewer and Kirby behind him, and knocked open the door without waiting for an answer. A man was sitting on the right-hand side of the bed getting undressed but stopped abruptly as the door burst open. He was about five foot nine, of medium build, and was just about to remove a pair of trousers which the detective immediately saw had been 'patched up.' His collar and tie was partly covered by a cardigan and a jacket, and a pair of boots were lying on the floor next to him. Confirming the man's name was John Healy, the policeman spoke.

'I am Chief Inspector Wensley of New Scotland Yard. I want to speak to you—' but the conservation was interrupted as Healy's wife arrived at the top of the stairs, shouting aggressively. Ignoring her, Wensley continued, 'It is inconvenient here. I must ask you to accompany me and these officers to Hitchin Police Station,' and he nodded towards Brewer and Kirby.

Healy asked, 'What is it all about?'

'I will tell you at the police station.'

Healy shrugged his shoulders, fastened his trousers, picked up his cap and went quietly, unhandcuffed, with the officers to the waiting taxi outside, which then took them to the police station. The detective was relieved the arrest had gone without incident and with no blood spilt. Waters was directed by Wensley to remain at the house until he returned.

With Healy safely at the police station, Wensley and Brewer now spoke to him, the senior of the two men asking the questions, the sergeant taking notes. The Irishman spoke calmly and offered no suggestion that he was aggrieved at being hauled out of his home but simply answered questions put to him and emptied his pockets willingly. Six £1 Treasury notes and some loose change was placed on the table and a cut to the prisoner's right finger occupied the police officers' attention. Slowly, Wensley told him why he was there and turned the questions to the detail of his movements on the night in question. When asked if he would make a statement, he said he would.

'I have worked for Kryn and Lahy Factory, Letchworth, for the past three weeks, prior to that I worked for Andersons, Henlow.

'I left Andersons on the Saturday and went into Kryn and Lahy the following Tuesday. I live in a furnished room.

'All my clothing except what I stand up in is at my address. I have made no purchase of clothing recently, neither have I had any given to me.

'I left off work the day I left Andersons, three weeks ago, at midday. I went home to 16, Radcliffe Road. I went out about 6 o'clock. I went to the Market to the Plough and Dial P. H. and remained until nearly closing time. I came away long before closing time. I think I would be home before closing time. I left between eight and nine pm.

'I can't remember meeting anyone there that particular time. I can't say what time I left there. I did not call on the way home.

'I have made a mistake. I left Andersons on Friday. I did not go to work at all on the Saturday. I can't say definitely whether I went straight home, but I think I did. I did not call on anyone.

'The scar on the first finger of my right hand I did about a fortnight ago, where I am now working. I can't say the day I did it. I was messing about with boxes and I fell in the snow. There were some persons there when I did it, but I don't know who they were. I was working all over the factory. I bound it up myself with a piece of rag in my pocket.

'I know Mrs Ridgley and had been there twice to make purchases. I have not been in the house for months.

'I did not have an accident or cut myself the Saturday after I left Andersons [25th].

'I did not give notice to leave. I was paid on Friday, the 24th January. I did not go to work on the Saturday but went and secured another job where I now am. I went to the Labour Exchange at Letchworth and they sent me to the firm. I was taken on.

'I went on Monday to Andersons to get my back pay. I went to my new job the next day.
(Signed) John Healy'[60]

Sergeant Brewer read the statement to him. Healy signed it.

Wensley spoke. 'You will be detained until some enquiry has been made regarding your statement.'

'All right, sir,' came the reply.

The detective chief inspector now carefully analysed Healy's account and identified a number of lines of enquiry he could pursue: his employers at Letchworth and Henlow, which would shed light on the prisoner's injuries; clothing and any other of his belongings in his room at 16 Radcliffe Road, which could be examined; and the licensee of the Plough and Dial public house in which Healy claimed to be drinking on the evening of Saturday, 25 January. Some of this could wait, he thought, for now it was crucial to return to Radcliffe Road, search Healy's room and interview his wife. He was sure he was chasing the right man.

Constable Waters was pleased to see his colleagues return. He had waited in the bedroom, which was cold. The fire wasn't lit and only a candle gave off a glimmer of light. He had convinced the Irish woman, who had calmed down and confirmed her name as Annie Healy, to wait downstairs. Wensley, Brewer and Kirby were now back with the bit between their teeth in search of unanswered questions. The chief inspector directed that the two constables remain in Healy's room while he spoke to his wife.

In the living room downstairs, she listened as the man from Scotland Yard explained about the murder of Elizabeth Ridgley and how her husband seemed to be connected to it. She now seemed almost accepting of the position she found herself in and spoke to Wensley answering his questions. She then made a written statement:

'We reside in a furnished room at 16, Radcliffe Road, Hitchin.

'I was married on the 13th August 1918 and have been living at my present address about two months. My husband up till three weeks ago to-day worked at Andersons, Henlow. He is paid on a Friday night. He did not go to work on Saturday 25th, he went as he told me to Letchworth to try and get another job, when he got back he said he had got another job. He got back just before 5p.m. He had his dinner and a wash and went out again. I cannot say positively what time it was, it might have been six or it might have been seven. He came back again about ten p.m. He was wearing the same clothes as he has now got on, his finger was cut, but I believe that was done in the morning, it was only a scratch. He was perfectly sober and did not say where he had been, he has not since told me where he had been that night. I cannot say whether he went out during the day on Sunday, but he went out on Sunday night. The patch that he has on his trousers he put on a fortnight or three weeks ago, it was on a Sunday. I have never repaired any of his clothing. I wash for the house generally on Wednesday, I wash his underlinen every week. He usually changed his linen on Sundays but this particular Sunday he did not change until Tuesday night or Wednesday morning. I have not washed those shirts and they are now in my room. He bought a new shirt because they were so bad and he did not intend to wear them again. I think he bought it at the outfitters shop in Bancroft Street.

'On Monday, 26th January 1919, he went to draw his back pay at Andersons and then went on to Letchworth but did not commence work until Tuesday, so he told me. The reason he said he left was owing to the reduced scale of pay. He usually went out every night but he has not been out this week of a night. He generally got home about 6 o'clock.

'I was an occasional customer at Mrs Ridgley's. I was in her shop between 7.30 p.m. and 8 p.m. the Saturday night she met her death. My husband has been in there several times with me to make purchases during the first six weeks we lived in Hitchin, that would be about August and September 1918.

'My husband usually got home about 9 o'clock or a little before. On the Saturday, the 25th, it was 10 o'clock when he came home. I wondered why he was so late, he did not tell me where he had been. We have no friends that we visit in Hitchin. I did not notice anything unusual about him when he came in, either in his manner or appearance. I was sitting in the dining room with Mrs Smith, May Smith, Jack Smith and Jens Christian Christiansen (a Dane). We stopped talking for about half an hour before we went to bed.

'My husband has always treated me kindly and I have got a great affection for him and would protect him if I could.

'My husband always keeps his money himself, he keeps it in his pocket. He gives me £1 or 30s on Friday night and if I want any more I have to ask him. He used to have a khaki handkerchief but I lost it yesterday, the 14th February, and I bought another one today.

'I bought the other one in Bancroft Street at an outfitter's shop. He used to wear the handkerchief round his neck when working at Andersons, but he left off wearing it when he went to Letchworth.

(Signed) With an X'[61]

There were a number of anomalies between the two statements, and certainly some more lines of enquiry opened up. Even before he started to search the Healys' room, Wensley knew that the main discrepancy centred around the time Healy came home on that Saturday night; he suggested sometime between 8pm and 9pm and his wife was very specific about 10pm. Both gave different accounts of the injury to his finger and Annie had implied that her husband had patched up his trousers on the day after the murder. This was consistent with Mrs Ridgley's dog attacking him. She also said that he had stayed in the same clothes for three or four days before he eventually bought a new shirt at the outfitters. He had claimed that he hadn't bought any new clothes. And why hadn't Annie asked her husband where he had been that night? If he had always treated her kindly, there would be no reason not to ask. If he really was as violent as Wensley suspected, was she too scared to ask? And how convenient was it that she had lost his khaki handkerchief only the day before he was arrested? All this fuelled Wensley's belief that Healy was the murderer, and he now relished the prospect of searching the family room.

Wensley's briefing to the two constables was barely necessary. They knew what they were looking for; anything that could link Healy to the murder. Sergeant Brewer was there to guide them anyway. The room was sparsely furnished, with a bed, a small table, a wardrobe and a chest of drawers, and it was this that Kirby searched first. In one of the drawers, he found three soiled men's shirts, one of which was 'very much bloodstained' and had the collar and tail torn off. Under some other clothes in the same drawer, he found the torn collar, itself bloodstained. The drawers were virtually empty, and pushed up in one of the corners he found the top of a pair of underpants, which had also been 'torn off.'[62] On top of the wardrobe he found a torn khaki handkerchief, and having examined the sheets on the bed, he found what appeared to be bloodstains and bundled them up. They would need to be looked at. Wensley quickly gleaned from Annie Healy that her husband slept on the side of the bed where the bloodstains were found.

Waters pulled out a suitcase from under the bed, opened it and found a broken triangular file which bore reddish-brown spots. He thought about the injuries to Ridgley's head and thought it sensible to take it; the marks could be blood. From the small table, he seized a bedtick (mattress cover), a tin box and a clay pipe, all of which appeared to have bloodstains on them. On top of the chest of drawers rested a collection of papers, which Kirby read, and he saw that they were Healy's army discharge papers and decided to take them. He was sure they would be of some use. Satisfying himself that the room could yield no more, Wensley and Brewer went back downstairs and spoke to the landlady, making sure that Annie Healy was out of earshot.

Annie Smith lived at the address with her eighteen-year-old daughter Mavis and son Bernard. It was clear they had something to say, and with Wensley ready to listen, Brewer pen and paper in hand, Annie spoke first.

She had seen articles in the newspapers, she said, about the death of Mrs Ridgley, and despite her nerves she forcefully put across that had she known earlier that the woman had been murdered she would have come forward. Wensley calmly, outwardly acknowledged this point, but on the inside his frustration bubbled. He had a feeling he was about to be told something that would have been very useful two weeks ago. He didn't let his emotions show and beckoned Annie to continue.

Apart from being the family home, Annie said, she used the spare rooms in her house to rent out to lodgers, mainly Irish labourers, and about two months ago the Healys came looking for lodgings. They had apparently only recently got married in Ireland and had come to England where he had got some sort of labouring job in nearby Henlow. Wensley sensed that Smith had a lot to tell and had to ask her to speak slowly and to take her time. She dropped her tightened shoulders, breathed a heavy sigh, took on a more relaxed and confident posture, and told the rest of her story.

Satisfied that they were able to pay their rent, she gave them a furnished first-floor bedroom at the back of the house. All her other lodgers were Irish and so they fitted in well. At first, they seemed a normal couple, him being the stronger in character of the two, with her almost deferential to her husband. They didn't speak much, she said, and their routine centred on John Healy working during the week and going to the public houses in town fairly frequently on his own, but occasionally the two of them would go out together to the pictures. Most evenings they would eat together in the house with the Smiths and the other lodgers.

Annie looked at her daughter as if looking for reassurance and got it in the form of a firm nod from Mavis. Annie cleared her throat and continued her story. As the weeks went by, John Healy started to come home drunk, raising his voice and threatening his wife. When cleaning the rooms, the landlady had noticed some damage to one of the walls and more than once had seen Mrs Healy nursing a black eye. On one occasion, Mrs Healy had been on the receiving end of such a severe kicking to her hip that she was unable to walk properly for a while and had spent the night downstairs sleeping on the sofa. Healy, she said, had turned into a very violent man with a terrible temper, leaving his wife scared at times to be in the same room as him. She had even confided in the landlady that she feared she would never 'die a natural death.'[63]

Wensley listened patiently, his sergeant taking down occasional notes as the story of what appeared to be common domestic traumas was laid bare, but his violent character was something he expected to hear. He held back on asking about what had been said in the letter he had received. Wensley's face gave nothing away.

The landlady paused for a while and gathered her thoughts. She continued, saying that just before Christmas 1918, despite Healy going out most evenings to the pubs, he declared that he had no money, and by the first week of January he was unable to pay his lodgings and fell into arrears. She also knew that the Healys were in debt to Mrs Ridgley, though Annie had gone into the shop the day the grocer was killed to pay some of it off. Wensley recognised this behaviour as normal – people struggling to make ends meet – and was beginning to see that the Irish woman was battling against her husband's drinking habit. Perhaps sensing that the detective was still wrestling with the purpose of the story, Annie Smith then came out with what he wanted to hear.

Getting confirmation from Wensley that Mrs Ridgley was last seen alive about 8.30pm on Saturday, 25 January, the landlady looked him in the eye and told him that John Healy was seen outside Mrs Ridgley's shop that night. She paused, allowing the information to sink in. Wensley, now clearly interested, asked in a quiet voice who exactly had seen him. Smith turned to her daughter, who until this point had been sitting quietly but listening to every word her mother said, and invited her to continue the story. The detectives turned their attentions on Mavis.

The eighteen-year-old was nervous, but she told her story with clarity, almost as if she had been rehearsing for this moment. On the Saturday afternoon, she had travelled to London by train and arrived back at Hitchin railway station at 6.45pm, where she was met by one of the lodgers in her mother's house, a Dane called Jens Christiansen. They had both walked back to the house in Radcliffe Road, had tea with John Healy and his wife and then went out again for the evening. They were returning home, and as they passed Mrs Ridgley's shop, she saw Healy – whom she referred to as Jack – 'standing just outside the shop at the corner of Garden Row where the railings joined the wall'. The time was about 8.20pm. She pointed towards him and said to Christiansen, 'There is Jack Healy.' As she said this, Healy looked at her but immediately turned away and started to walk slowly along Garden Row away from Nightingale Road. Mavis thought this unusual because he would usually speak to her. She and Christiansen walked home to Radcliffe Road, and when they got indoors, Mavis said to Annie Healy, 'I have just seen Jack standing at the corner of Garden Row.'

Annie had replied with a look of confusion and an expression of 'oh', and seeing her awkward response and wondering whether she had unwittingly stumbled across some sort of affair, Mavis quickly dismissed the subject and said, 'Perhaps he is waiting for someone.'

Mrs Smith then picked up the story, almost speaking too fast now for Brewer to be able to take his notes. She was at home that evening, she said, with Mrs Healy, who expressed concern that Jack hadn't yet returned and this was unusual for him, since he normally got home about 9pm. He eventually came in at 10.30pm, and instead of joining them in the downstairs living room, which was his routine, he went straight upstairs. She too had been waiting for this moment, and as if appreciating that it could be important, described the brown suit and grey cap he was wearing. She didn't see him again until the following morning, Sunday, when he was now wearing a bandage on the first finger of his right hand and saw that one or two pieces of skin were torn off the back of his hand. Healy came home, she continued, without Wensley daring to interrupt her, on the Sunday evening and Monday evening in a very drunken state, but the Saturday had been the only occasion that she could recall when Healy had come home late.

Mavis jumped back in. She was excited. Either on Tuesday, 28 January, or Wednesday, 29 January, she wasn't sure which, she actually asked Annie what had happened to Jack's hand, and she had replied, 'That is where he fell out of the chair and cut his finger.' Healy had in fact fallen out of a chair, she clarified, on the Sunday evening when he had arrived home drunk, but that was *after* she had seen his bandaged hand earlier that day. She sat back in her chair and stopped talking.

It was now Annie's turn again. She cleared her throat, drawing attention to herself. Healy started wearing clean shirts immediately after the Saturday and remembered Annie washing some of his other shirts later that week. She made sure Brewer was writing. Also, until the day before the murder, Healy had owed two weeks rent, twenty-four shillings, claiming he had no money, but on the following Friday he paid all his outstanding debts and paid a week's rent in advance – thirty-six shillings. Realising the significance of her last statement, and not wanting to pour guilt on the Irishman unnecessarily, she quickly pointed out that she had been led to believe, by Healy, that he had recently drawn his army gratuity pay that week of £8.10s.0d.[64] Perhaps that was why he had money, she offered. Both women now sat back in their chairs, and it took a while for Wensley to realise they'd finished their story. Mother and daughter just looked at the detectives.

Wensley was pleased. He had heard what he wanted to hear and more besides. His face gave nothing away. He had one question though. He needed to know whether Healy smoked. Yes, they replied in unison, and occasionally he smokes a pipe. Tobacco and matches, thought Wensley. Tobacco and matches.

As if wanting to get in on the story, the landlady's son Bernard wanted to give some information. Brewer gripped his pen again. He couldn't add much more but he said that at 7pm on the Saturday he was in the High Street when he saw Healy outside the London County and Westminster Bank. They spoke for about a quarter of an hour, and at that time, Healy had no injury to his hands. When they parted, Healy said he was off to Odell's to buy some cigarettes.[65] The sixteen-year-old then added that on the Sunday evening Healy had been playing a concertina in the house and he had watched his hands as they played the instrument. One of the fingers on his right hand was bandaged.

The four police officers returned to the police station, very satisfied that everything in the letter had been confirmed. The Smiths had been a crucial find, and they discussed how things might have been had the landlady and her family known the true circumstances earlier. Eager to follow up what the Smiths had said, Brewer went to see Healy in the cells and took his clothes from him so that Dr Spilsbury could examine them. He made a list:

> Jacket with blood spot inside right sleeve
> Vest
> Pair of trousers with blood smears in right pocket and two
> small tears, recent, back of right leg and patch over left knee
> Belt – bloodstain near buckle
> Pair of boots
> Pair of socks

Pair of pants
Cap
Handkerchief
Collar
Tie

The bloodstains were interesting, and the pants appeared to be new. Brewer remembered that a torn pair of pants had been found in Healy's bedroom, but the bottom half of them hadn't been found. It occurred to him that possibly the old pants had tear marks in them that would line up with the tears in his trousers, and Healy had thrown away this incriminating piece of evidence. But more importantly, when taking the clothes from Healy, the sergeant saw at close hand the injuries to his hand. It was a 'deep cut on the index finger of the right hand and a further wound or cut at the second knuckle joint of another finger on the same hand.'

Brewer explained what he had seen to Wensley as he was sitting at his desk running through the evidence in his head, making the occasional note. It wasn't a strong case, but, circumstantially, a picture was emerging that made it likely that Healy was the murderer. He knew that in order to convince a jury, he would have to show beyond all reasonable doubt that Healy was guilty, but he was confident enough to charge him and did so, accusing him of the wilful murder of Elizabeth Ridgley. After the charge had been read out, Wensley said to him, 'Do you wish to say anything in answer to the charge? You are not obliged to say anything unless you wish to do so but whatever you say will be taken down in writing and may be given in evidence.'

Healy replied, 'I know nothing about it, that's all.'[66]

Wensley now reflected on the injuries to Healy's finger and decided to get a doctor to make his own assessment. Doctor Grellett was to be called in again, only this time he would get a specific briefing from someone, telling him exactly what they wanted him to do.

Grellett came into the police station and examined the charged prisoner in the cell. He saw a series of injuries, including old scars and abrasions on a number of the fingers of his left hand. On the thumb and first finger of his right hand, there were more recent but nearly healed scars which were of a lacerated and penetrating nature. Grellett also noticed an abrasion on the back of his right shoulder and a bruise on the left of his back. Wensley was quite aware that Healy was a labourer by trade and would be expected to bear the marks of a manual worker, but he was intrigued by the more recent nature of the injuries to his right hand, consistent, he thought, with a dog bite. After asking Healy to remove his trousers, he noted two parallel abrasions on his left buttock.[67] His examination finished, the doctor said he was sure that the injuries he had just seen were consistent with dog bites.[68]

Moments later, Sergeant Brewer was back in the cell. Only this time he wanted the prisoner's fingerprints. Ten minutes later, with the Irishman's inked impressions pressed onto the Scotland Yard paperwork, they were hastily sent off for comparison with the marks on the cigar and cardboard box. It wouldn't be long now before the case was proved.

Chapter 17

Building a Case

The man from County Kerry appeared in court the following day, Tuesday, 18 February, three days after he was arrested and was formally charged with 'the wilful murder of Elizabeth Ridgley by striking her on the head with a blunt instrument between January 25 and January 27 at 125 Nightingale Road, Hitchin.' The journalists hung on to every word spoken in the crowded court, describing the proceedings as 'Hitchin murder charge' and a 'dramatic sequel to widow shopkeeper's death.' They described him as five feet seven and a half inches (1.72m) in height, of soldierly bearing, sturdy and muscular and with a stern, yet becoming, countenance. Clean-shaven, with a fresh complexion, he looked younger than his thirty-three years. He wore a dark mackintosh coat, closely buttoned to his throat, and appeared calm and self-possessed, answering without hesitation the only two questions addressed to him. Otherwise, he seemed apparently unconcerned with the gravity of the charge against him. Chief Inspector Wensley, addressed the seven magistrates, chaired by Mr W Tindall-Lucas, and informed them that Healy and his wife had been in the area for several months, employed in the erection of government-controlled works. Sitting in the back of the court, Annie Healy listened intently, she and her husband exchanging encouraging smiles. The detective continued to inform the court of the circumstances of Healy's arrest at Radcliffe Road, and when Tindall-Lucas asked him whether he had cautioned the prisoner, the detective replied, 'Not at that stage.'

Wensley was asked to elaborate further, and he detailed how a statement had been taken from him by Sergeant Brewer which had been read over to him and which Healy had signed in his presence. He described the wound on Healy's index finger and a further wound on the second knuckle joint of the same hand. When Healy was searched, he was found to be in possession of six £1 Treasury notes, three shillings in silver and one halfpenny. He added that at this time he didn't intend to submit to the court the statement the prisoner had made about the events on 25 January. He then finished his evidence, telling the court, 'That is all my evidence now and on that evidence, I ask for the case to be adjourned in order that I may place all the facts before the Director of Public Prosecutions.'

Tindall-Lucas turned to Healy and asked, 'Do you wish to ask any questions?'

'Not at present.'

'Have you any objection to being remanded for a week?'

'Well I do not see why I should be remanded at all.'

The chair of the bench conferred with his fellow magistrates and announced that the prisoner would be remanded for a week until Tuesday, 25 February, but expressed a desire for the case then to proceed.

'That is our wish and intention,' Wensley responded.

A small concourse of people waiting outside the court hoping to see a glimpse of the Irishman charged with the shopkeeper's murder was largely disappointed, as the taxi containing the prisoner sped off in the direction of Bedford gaol.

The resumed inquest the following morning was a disappointing affair for the journalists. They knew that the famous Spilsbury had been called in but his name was never mentioned at the remand hearing the day before – the inquest was probably where his evidence would be read out. Healy wasn't there and neither was Spilsbury, and Wensley merely advised the coroner that because of recent developments he requested a further week's adjournment so that the police could have more time to investigate and prepare the evidence. Shillitoe agreed and adjourned the matter. It was over in minutes.

Wensley now concentrated on filling in the gaps. Constable Kirby was proving a valuable asset to the investigation, and in an effort to make up for his earlier mishaps, he had already visited the outfitters shop in the town, where he showed the owners the bloodstained, and now partially ink-stained, handkerchief. Two shop assistants had examined it and were adamant that it didn't resemble those sold in their shop.[69] If Annie Healy had purchased one from there, which she claimed in her statement, it wasn't that one. Whether this helped in any way, Wensley wasn't sure, but he was pleased that Kirby had used his initiative.

Another matter which had been brought to Wensley's attention by Kirby was that staff at the Food Control Office had read about Healy's arrest and contacted the police station to report that his ration book had been handed in by some young girls on the morning of Tuesday, 28 January, the day after Mrs Ridgley's body had been found. The detective knew this was significant.

During the war, ration books had been crucial to people's very existence. They had been introduced by the government to address the increasing problem of people queuing for food with the inevitable consequence of stockpiling and preventing others from buying food essentials. Had rationing not been introduced, many thought the country would have turned to revolt as a means of avoiding starvation and anarchy would soon follow. Even though there had been over thirty thousand prosecutions for breaches of the food regulations in 1918 alone, the scheme was considered a success. Despite calls in the newspapers for the draconian measures to be curtailed and the role of the Food Control Office to be overhauled, rationing remained for many food items and the book was an important family document. Losing it was a big issue.

Wensley asked Kirby what else was known, and he told him that the clerk at the office had been unable to say who had handed it in, and more importantly hadn't asked where it had been found, but had said that a woman had come into the office a few days later and claimed it.[70] The address on the ration book was 3, Ickleford Road, and it was to this address he despatched his young detective sergeant. This was an important lead. Depending on exactly when and where this ration book was found, it could be the single most important piece of evidence. If it was found close to, or better still inside Ridgley's shop, it wouldn't look good for Healy. Anywhere else wouldn't help the case at all.

With all his staff fully occupied around the town taking statements, Wensley had time to sit back and build the picture in his head. He had taken a brief look around the area when he had first arrived, but now he had charged Healy, he wanted to go over the ground again. He wrapped himself up in his coat, scarf and hat and stepped outside into the cold air, crossed the road and took in the surroundings. Ridgley's home was a converted end-of-terrace Victorian house but now had all the hallmarks of an established shop. The sign outside advertising the grocer rattled in the strong wind blowing up Nightingale Road, and snow was beginning to thaw and fall from the roof. The blind covering the main shop window was a remnant of the war to ensure light didn't glow from inside to alert enemy bombers, but it had continued to serve its purpose for Mrs Ridgley as she was really not keen on schoolchildren sticking their noses up against her glass window. Metal advertisement boards were tidily displayed across the front of the shop; Sunlight soap, British Oak Shag, Rocklight lamp oil and Brooke Bond tea stood prominent. On the wall facing out over Garden Row, Cadbury's cocoa, Wills cigarettes, Reckitts Blue and Westward Ho!

smoking mixture was emblazoned. There was no doubt this was the place to go if you needed anything.

It was Garden Row he was interested in, and he crossed Nightingale Road and entered the slush-covered street. Ridgley's low garden wall was on the right-hand side, its back door facing out onto the thoroughfare, terraced houses facing opposite. This was the quickest route to Healy's house, and he wanted to be clear about exactly how close it was. Only fifty yards into it, he came across St Saviour's School, surrounded by its low iron railings. A gate opened into the school grounds. He walked through, turned to the right of the wooden building and directly in front of him was the rear of 16, Radcliffe Road, its passageway, as used by the lodgers, according to Annie Smith, on open view. Only a three-foot wall stood between him and the back of the house; Healy's bedroom window was staring directly at him. From one back door to the other was, at most, two hundred yards. The question was, once Healy had murdered Ridgley, what did he do? Assuming Ridgley was attacked around 9pm, he then had to make sure that both she and her dog were dead – probably the two or three thuds heard by the Roachs – and then search the shop for money, using only matches to see in the dark. He had to find time to bolt the front door to make sure he wasn't disturbed, open the till, steal the money and then find his way in the dark, lighting more matches, to the back door. Once there, he would have needed to ensure that no one in Garden Row was there to see him in the light of a nearby street lamp, climb over the short wall and walk home. The latest he would have got there would have been 9.15pm. Yet, he didn't get in until 10.30pm. So, where did he go? As he walked back along Garden Row, he thought through the options.

Healy would have been in pain, considerable pain judging by the rips in his clothing and the dog bites to his hand and buttocks, and he would have had a great deal of blood on him. Nothing suggested he was wearing a coat, though given the weather it would have been reasonable if he was. He would have needed to have gone somewhere to nurse his wounds, recover from the pain and try and wash off whatever blood he had on him. Where was he for that missing hour and a quarter? With no obvious answers, he returned to the shop to give instructions to Sergeant McBride. He wanted what he had just seen captured on camera.

While Wensley pointed out how he wanted the photographs taking,[71] Sergeant Brewer was having a cup of tea with Catherine Lawrence at 3, Ickleford Road. She was a spinster who lived at the address and rented rooms to people, quite often Irish labourers, who were employed in temporary work. Brewer asked her about the connection between John Healy and her address, and she told him that Mr and Mrs Healy had rented a room in the house in the six weeks leading up to Christmas 1918. They'd moved out, and she was at home on Wednesday, 29 January, two days after Mrs Ridgley's body had been found, when three young girls, the oldest about ten years of age, came to her house and showed her a ration book they'd found. The book was in the name of John Healy, of 3, Ickleford Road. Brewer asked her to think again about the date the girls had knocked on her door as he knew the clerk at the Food Control Office had been adamant that it had been handed into him the day before, 28 January. Lawrence became vague but settled again on the twenty-ninth. She wasn't to be convinced otherwise. Brewer allowed her to continue. She told the girls that Healy had moved, didn't know where he now was, and told them to take it to the local Food Control Office. George Brewer asked the obvious question – where and when exactly did they find it? Lawrence hadn't asked.

Thinking that he had dealt with the ration book issue, Brewer casually asked whether the landlady was able to provide any more information about the Healy family, but he wasn't expecting what he was then told. She poured out, almost with some relief, the bouts of violent temper displayed by John Healy and how he had repeatedly threatened her, as well as being violent to his wife. Gripped by this revelation, Brewer then asked if she had any knowledge of the Healys knowing or using Mrs Ridgley's shop, and she gave quite a remarkable answer. She related how, on 15 January, ten days before the murder, Mrs Ridgley had actually called at her address asking for the Healys, but by this time they'd moved and she had been unable to furnish her with their forwarding address. By chance, Lawrence was now aware of another address where the Healys had stayed since their arrival from Ireland and pointed the sergeant in the direction of Louisa Hawkins, who lived at 44, Nightingale Road. Brewer made a note.

Lawrence though, now eager to complete her story, explained how Ridgley had gone on to say that Mrs Healy owed her money and had recently been in the shop saying that she was no longer able to pay. John Healy had also been in the week before, around 11 January, but she hadn't confronted him about the matter as there were other customers in the shop and she didn't wish to cause any embarrassment. Catherine Lawrence shifted a little uncomfortably in her chair and, in a manner which demonstrated a deal of awkwardness, looked at the young detective and told him that she had advised Mrs Ridgley that she should confront Healy the next time he was in the shop and shouldn't be put off by his violent character. There followed a short pause while both calculated the significance of what she had said to Mrs Ridgley. Had her advice signed the shopkeeper's death warrant? This was almost certainly confirmed, Brewer thought, when Lawrence finished her story by adding that Ridgley had left saying that the next time the Irishman came into her shop, she would indeed confront him. Brewer took a statement from the landlady, and as she had it read over to her, the detective suddenly thought of another question. Asking generally about his clothing, he wanted to know whether Healy had possessed any handkerchiefs.

'Yes,' she replied, 'he had two good khaki handkerchiefs and one old one.' The detective added this to the end of the document, thanked Miss Lawrence, and left the house.

On his way back to Nightingale Road, where he was keen to tell his senior officer about what he had just found out, he made two further stops. The first was to see Louisa Hawkins, the other former landlady of the Healys, and she helpfully added two pieces of important information. Firstly, she had visited the grocer shop a few days before Mrs Ridgley was found murdered, and on being asked by the shopkeeper whether she knew the whereabouts of the Healys, she was able to say that they'd now moved to 16, Radcliffe Road. Perhaps, Brewer thought, this would ease Miss Lawrence's conscience; Hawkins had pointed Mrs Ridgley straight in the direction of Healy.[72] Secondly, she was in the shop between 5pm and 6pm on the day Ridgley was murdered, and that the shopkeeper was in fine spirits and good health. With the picture becoming clearer all the time, he then called in to the Plough and Dial public house in Bridge Street to speak to the landlord.

Brewer was fairly confident that Healy would be remembered in the public house, if indeed he had been there on the night in question. Doubtless, he would have been a regular there. Drinking was a big part of the culture of the working classes, a luxury, many would say, and before the war it had even been seen as a measure of a man's virility. The war, though, had to some extent changed that attitude; the social status of drunkenness had steadily fallen and was now regarded as rather squalid and ridiculous. But Brewer was right. Percy Gigg, the licensed victualler, remembered Healy well. He was a regular customer, drinking there at least five nights out of seven, and he described him as a reserved, steady man who had no friends and always came in alone. He couldn't say specifically that Healy was in his public house on the evening of 25 January, but it would have been normal for him to have been there. He was clear, however, that he closed the premises at 9pm, the normal closing time, and so could be certain he wasn't in there after that.[73] He was next in the pub at midday on the Monday after the murder; he was sure of that, as it was an unusual time for him to be there. Brewer thanked him and drove back to Nightingale Road to speak to Wensley.

Wensley's attention to detail was an attribute that had got him to where he was; thoroughness was the key, he used to regularly tell his juniors. Now, with Brewer sitting in front of him pouring out new information, his approach was paying off again. Healy's violent behaviour was interesting but he knew it didn't prove that he murdered Ridgley. What was of more significance was the fact that he owed money to the shopkeeper and had been in her shop more recently than he had said in his statement; that showed him to be a liar. But perhaps the most concerning piece of information was from the three girls who had found Healy's ration book within two days of Mrs Ridgley being found dead. Who were these girls and where did they find it? They needed to be found. He had an idea, but for now it must wait. Annie Healy was downstairs wanting to speak with the detectives.

Chapter 18

Keep Digging

Wensley knew that Annie Healy wasn't there to do her husband any harm. If anything, she probably wanted to try and show that he wasn't involved. But she had presented herself to him and a gentle approach was required. He invited the young Irish woman to sit down and he took time to take a closer look at her. The last time they had met was on the day he had arrested her husband and tempers had flared, although she had quietened down by the end of the evening. Now she was more relaxed. He had allowed her to visit her husband in the cells at the police station when he had been remanded in custody and it had been quite emotional. The couple had held each other and both had cried; the magnitude of the situation had hit them. He wasn't sure what to make of her, though. He knew she had a temper and was more than capable of hurling foul language around, but privately he empathised with her predicament and knew very well where she sat in the hierarchy of working-class life and how volatile the relationship was between her and her husband. Life would have been tough; crude economic reality would have meant any family money would have been put into a pot, and after the beer money was given to her husband, the breadwinner, there may have been just enough left for meat once a week. Her role was to keep the house, breed and bring up any children, not that there appeared to be any in this relatively recent marriage. Her somewhat puffed-up cheeks and confident grin masked, in his opinion, a troubled woman, and he was keen to hear what she had to say. Still wearing her raincoat and large brimmed hat, she looked at the man from London's famous Scotland Yard. He invited her to talk.

She wanted to make another statement, she said. She had things she wanted to say.[74] He would let her talk, but if he could he would try and get more information from her. She immediately took him by surprise, blurting out that she thought there was insanity in her husband's family. The detective suspected what was coming. She was going to make him out to be some sort of madman and not responsible for his actions. He let her

82

continue. She said his mother, although now dead, was 'at times not quite right' and his younger brother Tom, had been so 'funny' that the rest of the family had needed police protection from him. She added, 'My husband is sometimes strange,' but offered no more. There was a silence. She didn't go on to say, as Wensley thought she would, that if her husband had attacked Mrs Ridgley, he probably didn't know what he was doing. Ideally, he would have liked to have explored this further but knew he was trespassing on dangerous territory as he knew he could be criticised for trying to manipulate an important witness at a time when she was vulnerable. But, now that she was talking – she had come to him, he repeated to himself – he gently eased into the detail of Mrs Ridgley's death. He asked her about her husband's clothing and she confirmed that the two shirts taken away by the police belonged to her husband and that he was in the habit of wearing them both at the same time. They hadn't been washed since 27 January, the day Mrs Ridgley had been found. Pleased with what he heard he subtly switched the subject to the injuries to her husband's hand. Without hesitating, Annie said that on Sunday, 26 January, her husband had 'a scratch or something the matter with either the first or second finger of his right hand', which he asked her to bind up for him, which she did using a piece of her camisole. Normally he would go to church on a Sunday, although she couldn't now remember whether he did on this particular day. Asking her specifically about the evening before, the night of the murder, she said that she didn't ask her husband where he had been when he came home at 10pm, neither did he say anything.

Wensley knew what she was trying to do. She wanted to make sure she was being seen to protect her husband, but she had just confirmed her bandaging his wound on the Sunday. He asked her questions almost so casually that they must have appeared unimportant, but he cleverly teased out further pieces of information which helped to build a clearer picture. Annie told Wensley that on the Saturday of the shopkeeper's demise she had gone into her shop to pay off part of a small debt she owed, leaving her still two shillings in arrears. Later the same evening, she had been at home about 8.30pm when Mavis Smith, the landlady's daughter, and the Danish lodger called Christiansen had returned home, and being worried about where her husband was she asked them whether they had seen him. Mavis said that she had and he had been standing outside Mrs Ridgley's shop, though Annie quickly pointed out that Christiansen didn't recall it. Mavis then said that perhaps she had made a mistake and it wasn't him. Again, Wensley recognised this as her trying to taint what the Smiths had been saying to the police. Brewer quietly wrote down what Annie was now saying and Wensley put the questions to her. He asked about the ration book which had been handed in to the Food Control Office. She lost it, she thought, a couple of Saturdays ago, 8 February, and that it had been handed in, but when pushed for more clarity about the date, she was unable to give any.[75] He knew Annie was wrong about the date she had lost the ration book and that told him that this line of enquiry was even more important. The 'ration book children' must be found.

Annie had finished saying what she had come in to talk about. Her statement was read to her and she left the shop. Wensley was now even more convinced that Healy was the murderer, but equally he knew that Annie Healy's evidence would not be admissible in court as a wife could not be compelled to give evidence against her husband, but at least it would now be difficult for her to change her story and give evidence in any future trial.

But something else was nagging away in his mind. He talked it through with Brewer. He was trying to imagine the atmosphere that must now exist inside Radcliffe Road. The Smith family were clearly keen to speak about what they'd seen and how they obviously suspected that Healy had something to do with Ridgley's death. At the same time, the defendant's wife was living under the same roof and he was sure that words were being exchanged between them. Annie Healy had specifically mentioned that Mavis had been mistaken about seeing Healy that night and this could only have come from them talking between themselves. Wensley felt uncomfortable knowing that conflict was inevitable, and it was vital that if anything was to happen, every piece of information must be extracted from that household. He told Brewer that it was his job to keep going back to the premises to make sure that all was under control and to keep asking questions.

He did, and he found a household at war. The friction between the Irish tenants and the landlady's family was worsening, not surprisingly, Brewer thought, given what was at stake. He had needed to warn Annie Healy that if she continued to cause trouble, it could only do her husband harm. The Smiths continued to speak more about the Healy's washing regime in the house, and Jens Christiansen confirmed everything Mavis had said about Healy being seen outside the shop. More stories of violence between the Healys emerged, with John on more than one occasion threatening to kill his wife. She lived in total fear of him. At one point after the arrest, she had even broken down and said 'My Jack's a murderer. What shall I do?'[76]

It was these small comments which interested Brewer, and he found himself scribbling down pages of additional notes. When the news broke that the police were looking for a man with a wounded hand, Annie Healy had commented that 'I shall have to get Jack to take the bandage off. It looks rather bad for him. They'll think he did it.'[77] Between the murder and Healy's arrest, the family had been talking about how terrible it must have been for poor Mrs Ridgley to have been killed in such a way. Healy had jumped in, shouting, 'What was her life compared with the thousands of soldiers that have been killed? I have seen dogs walking about with pieces in their mouths.' And even young Bernard, the landlady's young son, recalled the Sunday after the murder when Healy's wife came downstairs in the afternoon and had said, 'Jack is up there and is washing himself all over.' They'd all laughed, he said, as it was very cold weather, there was no fire in the bedroom and no hot water.

Everything fitted. All these conversations were symptomatic of a man harbouring a guilty secret, and it was reassuring to know that after a dreadful start to the investigation, the right man had been charged. Justice would now take its course.

Chapter 19

Turning of the Screw

It was now Tuesday, 25 February, and Healy was back before the magistrates, only this time represented by George Passingham, a local solicitor who had been instructed by the Hitchin office of the National Federation of Discharged and Demobilised Soldiers and Sailors. The courthouse was crowded, with hundreds of people outside unable to get in. Healy, now somewhat paler after a week in custody, bore the same air of disinterestedness which had characterised his behaviour at the previous hearing and casually glanced from time to time at his wife sitting nearby dressed in her wide blue felt hat and fawn mackintosh raincoat. Though Wensley was present in court, on the advice of the Director of Public Prosecutions, the only witness to give evidence was Sergeant Brewer, who gave a detailed summary of the prisoner being taken to the police station, the taking of a statement from him, the searching of his lodgings in Radcliffe Road, the seizure of his clothing, which bore apparent bloodstains, the injuries to his finger, and that when Healy was arrested he was in possession of £6.3s.1½d.

Passingham rose and cross-examined the sergeant and immediately asked whether the prisoner had been cautioned at any stage during the taking of the statement from him.

'None at all,' Brewer replied.

'None of any description?'

'No.'

'Did the prisoner accompany you to the police station quite willingly?

'Yes.'

'Was he handcuffed?'

'No.'

In a manner as if to address everyone in the court, Passingham summarised this aspect of police procedure by putting into plain English that Healy had not been afforded the protection of being told that he need not say anything if he chose not to do so. Wensley knew what was coming. The law,

Elizabeth Ridgley's corner shop in Nightingale Road, Hitchin where she was found murdered on 27 January 1919. The rear gate and boundary wall face onto Garden Row. (Courtesy of the Mayor's Office of Policing and Crime and Hampshire Constabulary History Society)

The rear of 125, Nightingale Road, Hitchin taken from Garden Row. The rear downstairs window can be seen where Elizabeth Ridgley was attacked. The back door can also be seen through which the murderer escaped. (Courtesy of the Mayor's Office of Policing and Crime and Hampshire Constabulary History Society)

The rear garden of 125, Nightingale Road showing the scullery and kitchen. The harsh weather conditions are plain to see. (Courtesy of the Mayor's Office of Policing and Crime and Hampshire Constabulary History Society)

The view facing away from the shop with the houses in Garden Row (now demolished) on the left. (Courtesy of the Mayor's Office of Policing and Crime and Hampshire Constabulary History Society)

The alleyway which ran along the bottom of Elizabeth Ridgley's rear garden. (Courtesy of the Mayor's Office of Policing and Crime and Hampshire Constabulary History Society)

View from the passageway into the scullery/kitchen area. The back door can be seen on the left. The scales where the four pound weight was normally kept are on top of a barrel just inside the door. (Courtesy of the Mayor's Office of Policing and Crime and Hampshire Constabulary History Society)

The passageway leading from the front of the house to the scullery/ kitchen. The stairs led up to Mrs Ridgley's bedroom and additional storage rooms. (Courtesy of the Mayor's Office of Policing and Crime and Hampshire Constabulary History Society)

The passageway where the two bodies were found. The four pound weight, which was used to kill Mrs Ridgley and her dog, and the cigar box which the shopkeeper used as a till box can be seen resting on the floor. This photograph shows the scene which had been reconstructed by Constable Alfred Kirby under the direction of Detective Chief Inspector Fred Wensley. (Courtesy of the Mayor's Office of Policing and Crime and Hampshire Constabulary History Society)

The passageway leading to the front door of the house where customers would have entered. Note the blind on the inside of the door which would have prevented passers-by from witnessing the murderous assault. The shop entrance is out of sight to the right. The vast range of household goods that were sold in the shop can be seen stacked from floor to ceiling. (Courtesy of the Mayor's Office of Policing and Crime and Hampshire Constabulary History Society)

The rear living room where Ridgley was attacked. The bloodstained kettles and chamber pots on the floor were, according to Superintendent George Reed, the principle cause of Mrs Ridgley's injuries which led him to conclude that her death was an unfortunate accident. (Courtesy of the Mayor's Office of Policing and Crime and Hampshire Constabulary History Society)

Another view of the rear living room showing the huge amount of stock to be sold in the shop. The glass cabinet was spattered with blood. (Courtesy of the Mayor's Office of Policing and Crime and Hampshire Constabulary History Society)

The converted front room shop inside 125, Nightingale Road. Most household needs were catered for and would have been seen as a gold mine to any desperate criminal. (Courtesy of the Mayor's Office of Policing and Crime and Hampshire Constabulary History Society)

Behind the shop counter. The opened till-drawer contained the cigar box which was found next to Ridgley's body. The drawer and counter were covered in blood. (Courtesy of the Mayor's Office of Policing and Crime and Hampshire Constabulary History Society)

This fascinating photograph shows Nightingale Road in 1919. Elizabeth Ridgley's shop can be seen clearly on the corner of Garden Row with Frank Wheeler's shop on the opposite side. The entrance to Radcliffe Road, where John Healy lived with his wife, can be seen further along where The Gloucester Arms public house stood (today, it is Molly Malones). (Courtesy of the Mayor's Office of Policing and Crime and Hampshire Constabulary History Society)

The view from Nightingale Road along Radcliffe Road. Number 16, where John Healy lived, is a short distance along on the right hand side. It backs onto Garden Row. (Courtesy of the Mayor's Office of Policing and Crime and Hampshire Constabulary History Society)

The passageway at the side of 16, Radcliffe Road. According to the landlady, this was the main entrance used by the lodgers living at the address and would have been used by Healy on the night of the murder. In the photograph you can see a fowl house, immediately behind which, was a low wall giving access to St Saviours school grounds and garden Row. (Courtesy of the Mayor's Office of Policing and Crime and Hampshire Constabulary History Society)

The view down Garden Row along which Healy was alleged to have escaped. But where did he hide for an hour before returning home? The houses today no longer exist. (Courtesy of the Mayor's Office of Policing and Crime and Hampshire Constabulary History Society)

St Saviours School situated halfway between Mrs Ridgley's shop and Healy's lodgings at 16, Radcliffe Road. The photograph is clearly intended to demonstrate the ease of access between the two premises. The man standing in the school grounds is either Detective Sergeant George Brewer or Detective Sergeant Cooper who is looking in the direction of Healy's house. (Courtesy of the Mayor's Office of Policing and Crime and Hampshire Constabulary History Society)

The rear of Healy's house looking from Garden Row. (Courtesy of the Mayor's Office of Policing and Crime and Hampshire Constabulary History Society)

John Healy stands in the dock at Hitchin police court charged with the murder of Elizabeth Ridgley. On the left, seated at the table is Detective Chief Inspector Frederick Porter Wensley. The identity of the uniformed officer standing next to Healy is unknown but it is likely to be Police Constable 109 Alfred Kirby who discovered the bodies and worked with Wensley on the investigation. The police court was at the rear of the police station in Bancroft which is today used as a youth centre. (Hampshire Constabulary History Society collection)

Members of the public and service personnel wait outside Hitchin police station on 11 March 1919 awaiting the outcome of a remand hearing. The investigation and arrest attracted huge interest with barely enough room inside the court for solicitors and police officers. (Hampshire Constabulary History Society collection)

Eminent pathologist Bernard Spilsbury, who suggested the body of Ridgley should be exhumed for him to conduct a post mortem. His findings confirmed the theory that Ridgley had been murdered and she had not died as a result of an accident. (Hampshire Constabulary History Society collection)

The identity of this man is not known definitively, but it is probably William Augustus Craswell. It was his evidence that was at the centre of the police investigation. The photograph was probably taken in March 1919 at one of the remand hearings. Note the black armband, possibly out of respect for Elizabeth Ridgley. (Hampshire Constabulary History Society collection)

MRS. RIDGLEY.

This is the only known photograph of Elizabeth Ridgley which appeared in a newspaper article following her death. (Author's collection)

Nightingale Road, Hitchin.

The Woolpack public house, Starlings Bridge where ten year old Ernest Mansell bought a bottle of beer for Mrs Ridgley shortly before her death. The building no longer exists but it was only a short distance away from where Mrs Ridgley lived. (By kind permission of Simon Walker)

George Reed, retired police superintendent, relaxing in Great Yarmouth. There was nothing logical about how he arrived at the conclusion that Elizabeth Ridgley had died as a result of an accident. A previous murder investigation in which he had been involved resulted in him shooting himself in the hand with the murderer's weapon. (By kind permission of Jane Hanick – family collection)

Superintendent George Reed.
(By kind permission of Jane Hanick –
family collection)

Fred Wensley, then a detective inspector, at the Sidney Street siege in 1911.
He narrowly avoided death from a volley of bullets. (By kind permission of the
Bishopsgate Institute, London)

A young Police Constable Wensley at the time of his involvement in the hunt for Jack the Ripper. (By kind permission of the Bishopsgate Institute, London)

Wensley and his wife outside Buckingham Palace on the occasion of the award of his OBE. (By kind permission of the Bishopsgate Institute, London)

Wensley family gathering in happier times. Fred Wensley (back row on left), sons Harold and Frederick Wensley who died in the first world war (back row, third and fourth from left respectively) and wife, Lollie (front row, third from left). (By kind permission of the Bishopsgate Institute, London)

Edward Marshall Hall. He became known as the 'Great Defender' but on this occasion he prosecuted and the defendant was acquitted. (Courtesy of Sally Smith, author of *Marshall Hall: A Law unto Himself*).

Passingham argued, was quite clear on this point. No person ought to be made to incriminate himself and no police officer has any right, until there is clear proof of a crime having been committed, to put searching questions to a person for the purpose of eliciting information from him. If there is any evidence of an offence, a police officer is justified, *after a proper caution*, he emphasised, in putting questions to a suspected person in order to ascertain whether or not there are fair and reasonable grounds for apprehending him. Either the police suspected him or they did not. If they did suspect him, he should have been arrested and cautioned at the house and certainly before he was interviewed – which he wasn't. If they didn't suspect him, why had they taken him to the police station and searched his room? Passingham paused for effect and then suggested that of course they suspected him; the blood, the injured finger and a relatively large amount of money in his possession when he was searched at the police station all confirmed this. In Passingham's mind it was clear. The police should have arrested and cautioned him and he would have been less likely to have made a statement. Healy had been tricked.

Having made his point, Passingham now pursued the probity of the other evidence and asked about the conclusions in relation to the prisoner's clothing. The detective answered that he hadn't at that time received any report from Dr Spilsbury and one wasn't expected for some days – the pathologist was notoriously slow in producing his reports, though Brewer didn't share this with the magistrates.

His job done, Passingham turned to the bench and addressed them on a point of fairness. There was insufficient evidence, he argued, to justify a remand, and that he, Passingham, hadn't even been furnished with any information about the case. It was unfair, he continued, to remand Healy when the case was not seemingly being efficiently investigated.

The magistrates turned to Wensley, who had been sitting at a desk making notes, and asked him why he wasn't prepared to hand over the prisoner's statement to the defence. Wensley rested his pen on the table in front of him, stood up and looked at the magistrates. His calm, professional demeanour had a salutary effect. It would interfere with the course of justice, he said. He didn't want it to become public property until he had had time to investigate it, but then, almost as a peace-offering, he agreed to pass the statement to the defence for 'private use.' Passingham appeased, the case was adjourned until 4 March, but it was clear that, from this point on, the police evidence was going to be subjected to much closer scrutiny.

With another week's adjournment, Wensley now turned his attention to Healy's employers to see whether they could support his story about his movements, his earnings and whether he had injured his finger at work, as he had claimed in his statement. He despatched the enigmatic Constable Kirby to Messrs Andersons of Henlow and Detective Sergeant Cooper to Kryn and Lahy of Letchworth. Kirby was quick to establish from the chief accountant at Andersons[78] that Healy had joined the company as a labourer on 24 August 1918 receiving an average weekly wage of £3.8s.6d and had left their employ on 24 January 1919, the day before the murder. He had been paid £1.9s.11½d that day, although he returned on 27 January to collect a further £1.1s.6d which was owed to him. Kirby noted that Healy had only been paid a small final weekly wage as he had already that week asked for and had been given a sub of ten shillings, a fact which went, he thought, to support that Healy was short of money.

Meanwhile, staff at Kryn and Lahy were able to paint an interesting picture. The Irishman had presented himself to the foreman at the company on 27 January looking for work and the company was able to find his certificate of engagement,[79] which showed that he started work the next day, 28 January, and was taken on with an agreed wage deal of £2 a week, with further bonuses of twelve per cent plus an additional war bonus of 21s.6d a week. His last wage payment was on 19 February, when he was paid £3.14s.8d, which had been paid directly to Mrs Healy, since her husband by that time was in police custody. Cooper also established that when he was hired, the foreman saw no injury to his finger,[80] which the detective readily recognised as something which didn't support the developing theory that Healy had been bitten by Mrs Ridgley's dog during the attack.

Similar accounts were obtained from other labourers who worked with Healy in the weeks after 28 January.[81] To add to the confusion, two other workers claimed they saw an injury to Healy's finger on 6 and 9 February, a week or so later, when he had claimed he had injured it at work,[82] but the following day, 10 February, the bandage had been removed. One specifically stated that he definitely didn't injure his finger on 28 January when he helped him clear the snow. None of this added clarity to the saga of the injured finger, but one aspect which many of the workers at Kryn and Lahy agreed was that whenever the subject of the murder of Mrs Ridgley came up in conversation, Healy would walk away and take no part in it.[83] Not that it added much to the evidence, but Healy was also known to be a regular drinker at the Plough and Dial and Market public houses.[84]

Back at Nightingale Road and satisfied that he and his team had established a significant case against Healy, Wensley prepared a file of evidence and sent it to the Commissioner's Office at Scotland Yard, where his supervisor endorsed it. 'This case was handled with great skill and judgement and I have no doubt we have got the right man.' Another senior officer added, 'This reflects great credit on CI Wensley and I hope a conviction will result'.[85]

Both the local and national newspapers were following the story with relish, including putting photographs of Healy and his wife in their pages, and people started to come forward offering information, much of which was well-intentioned but added nothing of value.

That aside, all was going well, thought Wensley as he wrapped himself up to get warm while reading the statement just made by Nellie Ludford, who had turned up at the shop. She didn't think it would help very much but thought she would drop by anyway.

Brewer had interviewed her and he was now telling Wensley that he thought she was more important than she realised. On the night Mrs Ridgley was murdered, she had visited the shop and spoken to the grocer. It was at 8pm – she knew this as she heard the church bell strike – and had been speaking to Mrs Ridgley for about twenty minutes. During this time, nobody else entered the shop. As she left, the shopkeeper accompanied her to the front door and advised her to be careful not to slip on the pavement; it was now sleeting quite heavily, she recalled. Such was the weather, that Mrs Ridgley had commented that she was considering closing the shop at 8.30pm, half an hour before normal, as it was such a rough night. As Nellie exited the shop doorway, she turned left and immediately saw a man, a short man dressed in a bowler hat and dark clothes, walking towards her. Head down, she made her away along Nightingale Road and wasn't able to say whether the bowler-hatted man had entered the shop or not.[86] Brewer, who had taken the statement, thought about this for a moment. This was ten minutes before Annie Withey had had a conversation with the deceased but overlapped with the timings of William Craswell; hadn't he seen two men enter the shop about this time? Was the bowler-hatted man Craswell? The man who bought the tobacco and matches still needed to be found and Brewer wanted to get this tidied up. But it was now late and tomorrow was to be the final inquest hearing. Craswell would have to wait.

Chapter 20

The Inquest

The coroner, Mr Shillitoe, sat with a jury at Hitchin police court on 26 February and Healy, once more represented by his solicitor George Passingham, and with his wife sitting close to him, sat quietly in a chair at the side of the court, flanked by two police officers. It was now a month since Mrs Ridgley had been found, and people wanted to have answers. This wasn't a trial but an inquiry into the cause of death, but this was an opportunity for everyone, including the man charged with murder, to hear some of the evidence that may be used against him at any future trial. Healy had been advised by Passingham to remain silent. Any evidence given by him in an inquest would be admissible in the future; far better to reserve his defence if one was needed.[87]

Photographs and plans of the house were handed to the jurors and the khaki handkerchief and the four-pound weight were produced in court. To the delight of the crowded public gallery, Dr Bernard Spilsbury walked in, took his place in the witness box and began his evidence, knowing that his words would be printed the length and breadth of the country. With an air of superiority, he told the inquest that he had examined the exhumed body of Elizabeth Ridgley on 15 February at Hitchin hospital and went on to describe the wounds to the body, including the four on the back of the head varying from one inch to two inches long. Her nose had been flattened, there were cuts to her face and bruising to her arms, shoulder and right leg. Death, he said, had been caused through a haemorrhage of the brain due to the fracturing of the skull. Importantly, the cause of the fracture and the four wounds to the back of the head were by the same agent and at the same time and, he emphasised, they could not be caused by a fall and landing on the back of the head. The wounds were caused by a blunt weapon such as the bloodstained weight, a poker or possibly even the broken file which had been found by the police at Radcliffe Road. As her head was covered in thick hair, considerable force must have been used and, Spilsbury

90

asserted, the victim would have been lying face down when she received the blows to the back of her head.

The jury listened intently, and once he had given his evidence, they were asked whether they wished to ask the pathologist any questions. They did. Could the injuries have been self-inflicted? No, Spilsbury emphatically replied, and he added more information for the jury to digest. The dog had also died from multiple wounds to the head which had caused a fracture. In all probability, it would have been stunned by the first blow from a blunt instrument and finished off with a second. Referring back to Mrs Ridgley, he stated that it was likely that she passed in and out of consciousness for a while before dying and that most of her injuries were caused in the passageway of the house where she was found. One blow was delivered while she was standing in front of the glass cabinet in the living room and near the tins on the floor, and the bruises on her arms were probably defence wounds. The people in the courtroom listened in silence, before it was broken by the coroner thanking him for his evidence.

Since the inquest was to determine cause of death, medical evidence was crucial and formed the majority of the evidence to be examined, but a jury was now sitting in order to determine whether murder was suspected or not. To assist them, many of the witnesses identified by the police gave their evidence. George Rutland recounted the night of 25 January when he had mysteriously seen the light on in the grocer's shop, and the Chandlers told the jury about Mrs Ridgley's routine and how, although money had been found in the house, it was likely that the day's takings of Saturday, 25 January were missing. Next came the Smith family of Radcliffe Road, who outlined everything they had told the police about Healy; how he came home late on the Saturday night, the injury to his hand the following day, the fact he had no money and that Mrs Ridgley had even presented herself at the address with a bill for the Healy family. They spoke of how a few days later, Healy had managed to settle all his outstanding rent debts and on the Monday after Mrs Ridgley's body had been found he had bought himself a new shirt. One of his regular pubs was the Woolpack, a short distance from Mrs Ridgley' shop. Mavis Smith detailed again how she had seen Healy outside the shop and, in response to a specific question by Mr Odell, the jury foreman, she confirmed that the time was about 8.20pm that evening.

Next in the witness box was Louisa Roach, recollecting her hearing of 'blows and cries' coming from nearby, Wensley's description of her 'regrettable indifference amounting to callousness' appearing to ring true.

Her setting of the scene, however, was salutary, as Constable Kirby then described the carnage he had found on the Monday morning. He gave a detailed description of the inside of the shop, including the finding of the four-pound weight, although sheepishly he had to apologise for the now ink-stained handkerchief, which had totally obliterated the blood on the garment. The prosecutor, Francis Sims, listened carefully to what the officer said, and after a pregnant pause, and as if to create heightened tension, he asked Kirby to think back to the scene in the living room and posed a question.

'Was there also a bottle of beer?'

'Yes, sir,' and, recognising exactly what Sims was driving at, added, 'It had not been touched.'

The theory of a drunken woman falling over had been put to rest.

Inspector Warren now attended in the absence of Superintendent Reed and told the court that the khaki handkerchief and apron on the body had been saturated in blood and only a single spot of blood had been found on the deceased's shoe. Importantly, there was no blood nor evidence of dog excreta on the soles of the shoes, making it highly improbable that the victim wandered around the house for a while in a dazed and injured state. His evidence demonstrated that he did not now believe that Superintendent Reed's theory of an accidental death was likely. He was allowed to leave the witness box. Detective Constable William Waters, who had drawn the plans of the house, told the hearing that when he had searched Healy's bedroom he had found a broken triangular file, about nine inches long with red/brown stains on it in a suitcase under his bed, and on the mantelpiece in the living room an envelope addressed to 'Eally, Healy', which contained a bill for 4s. 7d. Six items had been listed. At the bottom, it read 'Settlement will oblige.' This was clearly Mrs Ridgley's attempt to get the money owed to her.

As William Goldsmith gave his evidence about the injuries to the dog, the jury seemed fascinated, even prompting one of their members, Captain Powell, to ask whether it was possible that the dog had first been struck, making it 'silly', thereby enabling further blows to be given. Goldsmith replied that he thought this 'was a very likely thing.'

The rest of the police witnesses took their place in the stand to tell their part of the story. Wensley spoke of the arrest, confirming the prisoner had attended the police station willingly, and that he had made a statement. He read it out loud, the court in total silence as for the first time details of Healy's movements on the night of the murder came out. In response to a question by Passingham, Wensley confirmed that the statement had been taken without a caution being administered. Next came Sergeant Brewer, who told the hearing that Annie Healy had now made two statements. Dr William Grellett spoke of the injuries to Healy's finger and scratches to his back and shoulder, saying the former *could* have been caused by a dog bite. Healy's previous employers provided information about his wages and how much money he earned but also commented on not seeing him with a bandaged finger. Finally, papers had been examined by the police that revealed that Healy had been discharged from the Royal Army Medical Corps in February 1916, where he had been described as 'character very good, honest, sober, intelligent, industrious and reliable and trained in first aid and ambulance duties.' Earlier military service had been with the Royal Munster Fusiliers and, upon his discharge in February 1906, his file was endorsed 'conduct and character very good'.

The witnesses' testimony given, and after what Wensley considered to be an 'unsatisfactory'[88] summing up by Shillitoe, the jury retired to consider the evidence. The coroner had ensured that the inquest had focussed on cause of death and paid little reference to Healy, who had sat passively throughout the hearing.

Wensley wasn't wholly surprised when the jury returned fifteen minutes later with a verdict: 'Elizabeth Ridgley came to her death by being murdered by some person or persons unknown'. If he could, Wensley would have thrown his head into his hands in disbelief, but he was too professional for that. He wandered outside, pleased that it had at least been proven that Ridgley was murdered, and took in the winter air. As he was deep in thought, three of the jurors approached him, conscious that their verdict hadn't identified Healy as the probable murderer, and told him that they were quite sure of Healy's guilt but given the coroner's summing up they were unable to return any other verdict, adding that they hoped this would give the police a freer hand.[89]

With the inquest over, the detectives were able to concentrate on the criminal investigation. Was there anything they had missed? Brewer remembered William Craswell and although he didn't see him as a priority, he wanted to speak to him again just to see if he could clarify what he had seen in the shop that night. On 3 March, he headed for 32, Kings Road and upon his arrival, the tailor seemed to be half expecting him and said that he presumed the detective had come because of recent events.

'What events?' Brewer asked.

Craswell explained that he had spoken to someone, a police officer he thought, about the murder but in fact the man had turned out to be a journalist. He had given the man information but once he realised the man's occupation he knew he had been deceived.[90]

'What information?' probed the detective, intrigued by this revelation.

Craswell continued, with Brewer casting his glare over the smartly dressed man, his bowler hat hanging on a hook behind him. On the night of the murder, he had been sent to Ridgley's shop by his wife to buy some bread. He had looked at his watch and the time was 8pm. He then walked to the shop, arriving about twenty minutes later, and just before he entered, a woman came out. Brewer knew immediately this must be Nellie Ludford and that the bowler-hatted man she saw must be Craswell. Without realising he was doing it, the tailor tightened and straightened his tie and said he went into the shop and was talking to Mrs Ridgley when the man he had mentioned in his earlier statement came in asking to buy some tobacco and matches. This man, he said, was John Healy. Brewer looked up immediately, amazed that Craswell hadn't mentioned this before. Recognising the impact of his statement, Craswell quickly added clarity. He didn't know it at the time, but on 26 February, he had seen Healy's photo in the *Daily Sketch* and immediately recognised him as the man in the shop buying the tobacco and matches. He had known him by sight for about three months, having seen him in various public houses, although on this occasion he was certainly not the worse for wear through drink. Realising the importance of this, he reported it to the man who had given the impression of being a police officer, only now he realised he had been hoodwinked.[91] Brewer was staggered that he had stumbled across this vital piece of evidence almost by chance and without any sense of urgency, but now that he had it, sixteen days after Healy's arrest, he headed straight back to see his chief inspector. He would be very pleased indeed.

Brewer strode up the stairs but was met by a forlorn-looking detective. Wensley came straight out with it; there were no fingerprints on the weight or either of the till boxes. Everything had been smudged, the result of so many people carelessly handling things. Something resembling the ridges and whirls which provide the uniqueness of human beings could be seen but all its detail was useless. Brewer grimaced as he sat down on the chair resting in the corner of the room. He knew that this was a setback, possibly a catastrophic one. Healy's fingerprint in blood on the boxes would have sealed the matter. But now it was gone. After a few minutes discussing the possibilities of Scotland Yard's experts re-examining the items and dismissing the prospect, Brewer suddenly remembered why he had rushed back. He told Wensley his news, and the initial impact was one of immense satisfaction, but as the information sank in, it dawned on them just how much better this would have been had Healy's fingerprints been found. Slowly, Wensley gathered his thoughts and with a sense of despondency he spoke. All witnesses who had already been interviewed should be seen again to ensure that nothing had been overlooked. Craswell said he had seen two men in the shop that night; who was the other one? He could be a vital witness.

The next few days were busy, speaking again to people who had already been interviewed, but from this trawl, only Catherine Lawrence, Healy's previous landlady, could add more. She had been asked specifically about Healy's behaviour and she repeated what she had already said, but added more detail. She had mentioned to Mrs Healy that a previous tenant, a Mr Walker, had left the lodgings without paying, and when Healy found out the two of them had been gossiping, he threatened the landlady with clenched fists, shouting that he would 'grind her bones under his heels and anyone else who got in his way'. She had also been told by Mrs Ridgley that Mrs Healy 'had a tongue on her' when she had challenged her over her unpaid debts at the shop and, still obviously regretting it, that was why she suggested to Mrs Ridgley that she should confront Healy himself over the debt.

Satisfied that as much evidence as was possible had now been extracted from his witnesses, Wensley turned his attention to Ireland and despatched Sergeant Cooper to the small town of Listowel in County Kerry. As the silence fell upon the corner shop, he shut his eyes and silently cursed Reed.

Chapter 21

Ireland Unearthed

Wensley wanted to keep the Irish angle out of the media limelight for the time being and the newspapers were merely able to report the retirement of Sergeant Boarder, one of the first officers to find Mrs Ridgley's body. He was described in the *Hertfordshire Mercury*, 1 March edition, as a 'courteous and painstaking officer' and if that was so, thought Wensley, why hadn't he thought to challenge Reed's original conclusion? Perhaps he would never know. But apart from stirring up perhaps false excitement with the news that a Scotland Yard officer was travelling to Ireland, there was another reason why Wensley wanted this particular enquiry to be kept quiet.

Ireland was politically volatile. There was a great sense of ill-feeling between those seeking, and those opposing, the British government's hold over the island and many had died during the last few years as political tensions had increased. Wensley was very aware that, only recently, two Royal Irish Constabulary constables had been murdered by the IRA, and he had also been briefed that two men had just been charged with smuggling guns to Ireland who had been found in possession of fourteen revolvers and a Sinn Fein membership card. And now, here he was, sending an English police officer to a Catholic stronghold in County Kerry to make enquiries about a war veteran accused of murder in England. He didn't expect a good reception.

Listowel was a small rural town, and the thinly populated locale of Clievragh, where the Healy family lived, was two miles to its north. In company with officers of the Royal Irish Constabulary from Listowel barracks who knew the family well, Sergeant Cooper headed for the small cottage in the corner of the field, well briefed on the violent reputation of the family. They knew all about the mad mother who had died six years ago, John Healy's drunken brawls with his brothers and his incessant ramblings about the war.

But there was no confrontation. Cooper sensed that, as he explained to Healy's father why he was there, his sudden appearance on the doorstep had been somehow expected. Michael Healy spoke freely about his son's background. He had been educated at the Listowel Convent Infant and National School, leaving at the age of fourteen years old able to read and write and had worked on local farms until the age of seventeen when he joined the army in February 1903. He enlisted at the barracks in nearby Tralee and joined the Royal Munster Fusiliers, whereupon he was posted to Gibraltar for three years. After three years in the Kerry militia, he returned home as a Reserve, where he resumed work as a casual farm labourer. At the outbreak of war in 1914, he was sent to France with the First Expeditionary Force, but in 1916 he was wounded and thought he had been invalided out of the army, although Sergeant Cooper knew already that this was not strictly true.. He returned home and soon after went to Scotland and obtained employment in a munitions factory. As far as he was concerned, his son then moved to somewhere near Lincolnshire[92] and remained there, rarely coming back to Ireland other than to marry, he thought, in September 1918 (it was in fact August).

The father confirmed everything about his own wife's insanity and subsequent death but then started talking again about his son's behaviour after he came out of the army. He had started to drink heavily, he said, although dismissing it as normal behaviour, but he often acted strangely, going for long walks without talking to anyone and threatening people without provocation. More worryingly, he brought this unbalanced behaviour into the family home, and he told about when he had been given a black eye, how there had been threats to burn the house down, how his other son had needed to smash John over the head with a set of tongs to calm him down, and about the routine smashing of windows in the house. The Metropolitan officer had already been told most of this by the local constabulary, but it was good to have it all confirmed by the father. He now had a pretty good idea of who they were dealing with and could see how this quite extraordinary behaviour fitted into Hitchin and how Elizabeth Ridgley probably met her death. He could imagine the Irishman leaning over the shopkeeper, drunk and with no emotion, smashing the four-pound weight down onto her skull as she lay helpless on the floor. The dog would have been an easy kill.

He had three more family members to see while they were in Ireland; Healy's sisters, Hannah Healy, Margaret Healy and Bridget Cooney. Hannah and Margaret had little to say other than they had become aware of their brother being arrested for murder after a letter had been received from Annie Healy, who told of the arrest. Bridget, on the other hand, told him something of importance. When asked about any contact she had had with her brother, she stated that since Christmas 1918 she had sent him three parcels,[93] each containing 1lb of butter and 1lb sugar. She had made no arrangements with him about payment, but around 2 February, less than a week after the murder, she received a registered envelope from him containing a ten shilling Treasury note, accompanied by a letter from John saying that the money was in payment for the butter and sugar. Before any excitement rose too high, she quickly added that she had destroyed the letter the day she had received it and had spent the money. Here was more evidence, thought Cooper, that Healy was in possession of money shortly after the murder. She confirmed that she had been told of her brother's arrest by Annie Healy in a letter she had written to her on 18 February, three days after his arrest,[94] but this time, she still had it. Cooper read it with anticipation.

> 'Dear Bridge,
> 'its with a sorrowful heart I sit to write you this terrible talle. About three weeks ago last Saturday there was a woman and her dog found dead in her little shop after been brutealy murdered, robbery having been the motive. Since then there has been dectives from Scotland Yard searching through Hitchin for the murderer but without avail. On last Saturday night Jack came home from work as usual about six o'clock had his dinner we both went to our room and Jack had a wash and shave we had a talk we decided not to go to the pictures as Jack was to work the next day sunday. About eight he went for a drink he came back soon after and went to bed. I was sitting by the fire with the landlady and her son and daughter about nine o'clock when the front door open and a dective and poliseman came rushing in at the same time two came rushing through the back door the landlady asked what was up, they said they wanted a tall dark man wearing a wounded stripe and a rag in his finger they then asked if they could look through her rooms they went up stairs the first room they entered was Jacks he was in bed they told him get up and dress, he says what is it all about they told him they were arresting him for the wilful murder of this woman. After taking him to the barrack he had to make a statement they afterwards came back to me I had to

make a statement also Mrs Smith and her son and daughter, they then went up stairs to our room and made a search they took with them the sheets of the bed my nightdress and some old shirts of Jacks. I went to see him three times on Sunday but I would not be allowed I also went several times yesterday but there was no chance for me to see him, I then went about eight o'clock to the dective last night and he took me to poor Jacks cell there he was sitting on his old bed dressed in convicts clothes he felt ever so bad, when he saw me we both cried until I was brought away. There was a special court held on him today and he was remanded until next Tuesday I was allowed to the court and after I was left go with him to his cell for a while of course there was a policeman with us at two o'clock today he was sent to a plase called Bedford sixteen miles from here I was left see him to the train I gave him some things, but just now the police brought them back to me again he would not be allowed keep them he went off in very good spirits he says we can rest assure he will be out again as he is perfectly innocent of the crime. I would not write you this terrible news but Jack told me do so I will not write to my mother until I hear from you again. They took Jacks fingerprints to see if they would correspond with bloody finger marks they found in a cash box and on her till and also on the bolt of the door they also took his clothes from him and sent them to Scotland Yard to be annalised they searched him and took his money from him he asked to have it given to me today but they refused. I dont feel I can say anymore now hoping to hear from you as soon as possible, I remain your broken hearted Sister Hamie.

'only on Saturday night we were talking of our future little home. Bridge keep this very quite as long as possible.

'Jack had six pounds found on him but I had got no money then.'

The letter gave a very clear picture of how Annie was dealing with the situation. Barely had he finished reading it though, when Bridget produced another, again written by Annie, this time on 26 February, the day of the inquest verdict. The detective, not believing his luck, read it.

'Dear Sister,

'It is with a sore heart I write you this. Jack was brought to Hitchin on Tuesday morning and his case went on all day *tuesday* and *Wednesdays* and he is again remanded untill next tuesday. He will be tryed here again and if he is not left off then, he will be put back again untill next June and what will we do then. I am in a very bad position now living here with those people that are trying to swear my husbands life away. God Bridge I cant have patience, fancy the bitch of a landlady and her son and daughter to go and swear as falce as Hell against him. They are crying for blood money but Bridge they have not it yet. God is good and all powerful, we will wait and see they may be sorry yet. Poor Jack went back to Bedford today, we had a good time together in his cell while he was here I brought him all his food and the Hitchin police were very good and kind to him, his own clothes were taken from him, but the inspector of the police gave him a very nise suit of his own servis. Jack's photo and mine appeared in the Sketch today it will be in next sundays paper I will get one and send it to you.

'for God's sake Bridge pray as hard as you can for poor Jack, I am getting Mass said for him I will also go to Holy Comunion and pray that God will clear him of this awful charge. Oh God Bridge fancy Jack and I sitting there in court and listening to people going up and trying to swear his poor life away. I will almost go mad I cannot bear it much longer. I will say good night now Bridge and pray to The Almighty for Jacks release. I have got a very good solicitor.

'Dear Bridge write by return and tell me what shall I do.'

These were powerful letters, not from an evidential point of view, but it showed how Annie was dealing with the situation. Everything the detectives had learned to date told of an unbalanced, violent Irishman who had ruled his wife with a rod of iron, a woman fearing for her own safety, yet these letters showed a woman who was blissfully ignorant of the possibility that her husband could be a killer and, despite all the violence that had been meted out to her, cared very much for the man now charged with murder. It was clear that her genuine belief, her faith, would see her and her husband through this traumatic period, but in reality, she was at a loss as to how to deal with the situation. Was she a woman capable of shielding a murderer or did she genuinely believe her husband was the target of unjustified persecution?

After a visit to John McKenna, a farmer who had employed Healy as a labourer who told of his propensity to viciously and unnecessarily thrash horses, Cooper telephoned Wensley to update him, packed his bags and set off back to England. He had unearthed a man who had returned from the Western Front an unbalanced and violent war hero.

Chapter 22

The Evidence is Tested

Healy's previous appearance at the magistrates' court on 25 February, with little evidence being tendered, had put extra pressure on Wensley to declare when he would be ready to proceed. He had told the court that as soon as that stage had been reached he would produce witnesses in order that they could be cross-examined, and it was suggested to him that the following week, 4 March, some of these witnesses would be expected to appear. Wensley was still visiting and revisiting important aspects of the investigation and wanted as full a picture as possible to be presented, but he knew he could delay no longer. The day had now arrived and Wensley looked at what he had.

Healy had a motive; he had no money before Mrs Ridgley's death, had debts, and managed to pay them off afterwards. He had the opportunity; he was seen outside and inside the shop immediately beforehand. His story of where he was that night was, at best, vague, at worst, 'an absolute failure to account for his movements'[95] and at variance with his wife's account. The Irishman was also seen nursing an injured finger on the days after the attack, had torn clothing, and injuries to his body that were all consistent with dog bites. He also owned three khaki handkerchiefs, one of which had been 'lost' by his wife. Spilsbury, Roach and Goldsmith would be more than able to demonstrate how likely it was that the attacker had been savaged by the dog, and blood on his clothing supported the case that he was the man that violently and callously attacked the shopkeeper and her pet. Finally, the evidence he had obtained from Ireland would show him to be a violent and unbalanced man, although whether this would be allowed to be put before the court was yet to be seen.

Spilsbury, though, was not yet ready to give his evidence. He was still analysing the material and was busy in other trials; his availability was limited, but at least Wensley could introduce other witnesses who were ready to testify. He briefly mused over the fact that there was no fingerprint evidence, something which so easily could have been avoided, and thoughts echoed around his head that had he been called in earlier he would have been able to have presented a stronger case. But there was no point in dwelling on it. He had to go with what he had. The newspapers didn't yet know about Healy's previous violent behaviour and he wouldn't be in a position today to inform the court as Sergeant Cooper was still travelling back from Ireland and he wanted to be able to scrutinise this new evidence before it was read out in open court. Importantly though, due to the unscrupulous behaviour of an unknown journalist, did an editor somewhere know of Craswell's epiphany and that he would now say that he saw Healy in Mrs Ridgley's shop on the night of the murder? It wasn't the strongest of cases, but on balance, the pressure to start outlining the evidence necessitated him being prepared to make some of it public.

The police court in Hitchin was again packed, with barely sufficient space to accommodate those who needed to be there. The case had gathered interest since the arrival of the Metropolitan detectives and particularly so since the arrest of Healy, and everyone knew that the time had come for the police to start making their case. They wanted to hear the details, and newspaper reporters crammed into the small room. Healy was dressed wearing a close-fitting blue suit and a soft collar and tie. His wife sat at the back of the court; the gathered masses gazed at her. The same chairman of the bench, Tindall-Lucas, presided, and alongside Wensley sat Chief Constable Law, the man who had reopened Reed's investigation. He looked solemn, doubtless masking a sense of nervousness as his judgement was effectively to be put under the microscope. Francis Sims, the middle-aged Principal Assistant of the Director of Public Prosecutions, prosecuted, his slim, balding figure projecting a sombre atmosphere in the court. George Passingham again represented the defendant.

As the prosecutor stood up to address the bench, a hushed silence fell about the courtroom. He gave a very brief overview of the case, summarising Healy's presence in Hitchin, the fact he owed money and was aware of Mrs Ridgley and her habits. He described the scene inside the shop, the location of the body, and suggested that the khaki handkerchief around the deceased's neck had probably been used as a gag. After handing out the plans and photographs of the house, he outlined how the blood-splashed till was empty, detailed the rest of the blood in the house and read out Healy's statement. He then called his first witness, Mrs Ridgley's sister, Mary Chandler.

The deceased's relative spoke quietly about her sister's life and described her Irish terrier, Prince, as 'one of the best'. As she spoke, the spectators' stares moved from her to Healy as he was allowed to sit down and was provided with pen and paper. Resuming, she described the inside of the shop, explaining that the place appeared untidy as her sister had taken delivery of many goods the day she met her death and hadn't had time to put them away, including a selection of savoy cabbages and tinned and enamelled goods all wrapped in brown paper. She described her sister's routine of tallying her till at the end of each day and, referring to the cigar box and treacle tin in the photographs, told the court that these items were always held in the till. She estimated that, typically, on a Saturday, her day's takings would be somewhere between £10 and £12. When asked about how she had found the shop once it had been handed back to her by Superintendent Reed, she said there was blood everywhere, including on the brown paper in which the saucepans had been wrapped. Distressed by such a sight, she had cleaned the place and burned the paper. She had set the scene well. The next witness took the court by surprise; it was William Augustus Craswell.

Craswell confidently told the court that he had gone to Mrs Ridgley's shop at about 8.10pm on the Saturday evening and spoken to the deceased, something he did most Saturday evenings. The lamp was on in the premises and he stood speaking to her for quite a few minutes. While he was talking to her, a man came in and bought some tobacco and matches. At this point, Sims asked him, 'Have you seen him since?'

Craswell replied, 'Not until today.'

'Is he in court?' Sims asked.

The reply resonated around the court. 'He is the prisoner.'

Healy reacted. He jumped up, pointed to himself and screamed out, 'Me?' He continued to shout out an unintelligible rant before he was quietened by Passingham. Craswell was allowed to continue and he told the court that Healy left the shop before he did, and then he added one more piece of vital information. While he was in the shop, Mrs Ridgley appeared 'jolly' and he had stroked the dog. Asked what the deceased had been wearing, he said that she had nothing around her neck but was wearing a dark blouse with a fancy collar. Closely cross-examined by Passingham, Craswell changed the time of him being in the shop to 8.15pm, and other than the fact that he could recall Healy wearing some sort of hat, he couldn't say whether or not he was wearing an overcoat, though he confirmed it was 'a bad night and cold'. As Craswell left the witness box, murmurs could be heard about the court.

After George Rutland gave his evidence about seeing Mrs Ridgley's shop unusually still open just after 9pm, and Gertrude Day telling of not being able to gain entry into the shop on the Monday morning, Louisa Roach spoke of the noises she had heard the previous Saturday evening; the thuds, the barks, the groaning going on into the night. She was followed by Constable Kirby, who described the scene again in great detail, the finding of the bodies and how he had searched Radcliffe Road when Healy had been arrested, and found, among other things, part of a khaki-coloured handkerchief.

The witnesses had taken all day to give their evidence and be cross-examined, and Wensley informed the hearing that Dr Spilsbury would be expected to give evidence next week. But he wanted to keep the momentum and explained he was pursuing the identification of three young girls who had found Healy's ration book and had handed it in to the Food Control Office. He didn't tell the court but he had already sent Brewer back to see Catherine Lawrence to see if she could add any more detail about the schoolchildren, but despite the sergeant dragging her round every school in Hitchin to see if she could recognise them, she couldn't, and could offer no more. The hearing was adjourned until 11 March and Wensley briefed the hungry journalists. An entry appeared on 8 March in the *Hertfordshire Express:*

> 'MURDER MYSTERY AND A RATION BOOK. It will be remembered that a lost ration book belonging to the Healys has been mentioned in connexion with the Hitchin murder mystery. Three schoolgirls are said to have found the book and taken it to 3, Ickleford Road, where the Healys lodged before moving into the Radcliffe Road apartments. They were apparently eventually asked to take the book to the food office. Chief Inspector Wensley is desirous of discovering the three girls who discovered the ration book at the end of January and he will be grateful if the parents will communicate with him at 125, Nightingale Road.'

Satisfied that his advertisement would bring the girls forward, he returned to Nightingale Road.

Meanwhile, Kirby had been working hard and had found another outfitters in the town who sold handkerchiefs. Armed with the ink-stained fabric, he paid the shop a visit. The woman who worked there proved most helpful. She was shown the handkerchief, confirmed that she sold that particular style, and remembered a man coming into her shop at 7pm one Saturday evening, sometime in the middle of January, and buying two. She was able to vaguely recall him, and Kirby asked her to come to the police station with him to see if she could recognise Healy. She looked at the prisoner in the cell and said that, although he looked similar, she couldn't be sure.[96] Boosted by this development, he visited a tailor's shop owned by William Rowe, and the owner quickly recalled selling a man a shirt identical to that owned by Healy on 27 January and another one a week later. He remembered the date specifically as his wife had been ill. Rowe had also now seen Healy's photograph in the newspaper and positively stated that it was the same man. Kirby felt pleased. He had identified the source of the shirts and probably identified the source of the handkerchief.

By the time the following Tuesday came round, Spilsbury had completed his analyses and had prepared his report. He was ready to outline his findings to the magistrates but had to wait his turn as Sims had lined up six other witnesses who were available and ready to tell their part of the story. This was Healy's fourth appearance, and again, during the hearing he was allowed to be seated, making notes on a piece of foolscap. The court was once more packed with an insatiable public, barely allowing room for the lawyers and police officers. Healy's wife sat on a seat at the back.

William Goldsmith spoke clearly and dispassionately as he described the injuries to the dog. 'Two or three blows,' he said, had been inflicted to the head, causing it to fracture, and there was no evidence of it being poisoned. His evidence was short but, thought the prosecution, would go to show that the attacker of the dog and the shopkeeper were one and the same and fitted well with Roach's evidence last week of the thuds and barking.

The next witness was vital, and as she spoke, the spectators' subtle and almost indiscernible glances shifted between her and the defendant. Annie Smith, who had been the person to first bring Healy to the attention of the police, appeared calm. She described her house and how the Healys had been lodging there over the past few months and how all her lodgers entered the house using the passageway down the side of the house. Recalling specifically the night of 25 January, she stated that at this time he owed two weeks rent and he left the house at 7pm. At this point she told the court that the clock in her living room was always half an hour fast; that's how she liked it. But she was sure about all her timings.

She continued with her story. His wife, Annie, remained at home. He returned at 10.30pm and walked straight up to his room without speaking, although as a general rule he would have a cup of cocoa or Bovril before retiring to bed. The following morning, his wife took him breakfast in bed, but when she did see him later in the day she noticed 'that he had a piece of rag bound round the first finger of his right hand,' something that hadn't been there the night before.

Wensley listened closely as she spoke. She was probably one of the most important witness in the whole case. Other people each brought their part to the story, but Smith was crucial. He knew that this was only a remand hearing and the prosecution only had to show that there was a prima facie case against the defendant so that the magistrates could be satisfied Healy could be sent for trial, but he focussed on her every word. Would she waver from what she had said in her statements? She was asked whether she had enquired about how he had got this apparent injury, and she replied that she had. Healy had said that he had 'knocked it'.

Good, thought Wensley. The magistrates would at least now know that Healy hadn't denied having an injury. Smith was doing well.

She now continued about the following Monday, the day Mrs Ridgley's body had been discovered. Healy, she said, had bought a new shirt and pants, and towards the end of that week had bought another shirt. He had even asked her whether she could make use of his old pants.[97] And then she came out with the bombshell. She told the court that Healy used khaki handkerchiefs. Magistrates looked down and made notes, the public looked wide-eyed at each other, journalists scribbled. Finally, she told about Mrs Ridgley coming to her house with a bill for the Healys, making the point that they were in debt to the woman who had been found dead. Smith was asked a number of questions by Passingham but she stood her ground and didn't deviate from her evidence. She was then allowed to leave the witness box.

Next came her daughter, Mavis. She spoke of seeing Healy outside the grocer's shop at 8.20pm, adding that she had mentioned this to Annie once she had got home and how she had seen that this had been a bit awkward and changed the subject. The prosecutor Sims raised his hand to indicate for her to stop talking. He had a question.

'Why did you tell Mrs Healy that perhaps it was not her husband who was standing near the shop?'

'I knew Mrs Healy was jealous of her husband. I thought probably she might think he was waiting for a girl.'

'Have you any doubt that it was Healy?'

'I have no doubt at all.'

Having got the point home, he called his next witness, Christiansen, who simply confirmed seeing Healy outside the shop and that his finger was bandaged the next day.

The public could now be seen to be getting restless as they waited for the famous Bernard Spilsbury to give his evidence. He had already spoken at the inquest, but this was somehow different. These were now criminal proceedings which could lead to a man being hanged. They had to wait a little longer though, as Healy's previous employers spoke about not seeing Healy with any injury but added that neither had Healy reported any injury to his finger which had been caused at work, something which he would have been expected to do.

And now, as if being left to last for effect, Spilsbury slowly and confidently walked into the witness box. He informed the court of his qualifications and experience and then, having been asked to describe the injuries to Mrs Ridgley, he methodically went through each aspect. After a description of the fifty-four-year-old woman and her general appearance, a standard prerequisite, Spilsbury launched into the nub of the matter. There were two fractures to the skull and numerous wounds and bruises. The bones of the nose and lower left jaw were fractured and the weapon used to inflict these wounds was a blunt one with 'not a very striking surface'. The clerk of the court handed the four-pound weight to him, which had been openly displayed on the table in front of the magistrates, and asked his opinion as to whether this could have caused the injuries. His opinion was that the wounds 'might' have been caused by the weight, but if it was, the deceased must have been lying face downwards on the ground when the injuries were inflicted. As he had outlined during the inquest, he pointed out that the body bore self-defence bruising and the injuries to the top of her head were consistent with the deceased at some stage being dragged by the hair while she was still alive. A loud gasp echoed around the courtroom. Suddenly, the violence to which Mrs Ridgley had been exposed was brought home in sharp focus.

Turning to the clothing that had been shown to him as belonging to Healy, he said he had found a small bloodstain on the right sleeve of his jacket, a number of bloodstains in the right and left trouser pockets, smears of blood on the sheets from the prisoner's bed and bloodstains on three of his shirts; all of it was human blood. Finally, he said in answer to a question from Passingham that there was no blood on the broken metal file which had been found in Healy's bedroom. The impact of Spilsbury's evidence reflected the two hours he had spent delivering it; everyone held onto every word. He left the witness box, everyone's attention following him.

The purpose of the remand hearing was to test the evidence, and it was for the prosecution to show that there was a case to answer; the defence had to prove nothing. Passingham didn't ask Mrs Healy to give any evidence, but despite him having no obligation to do so, he did produce a witness. Another of the lodgers at 16, Radcliffe Road, McCarton, told the court that he had come home drunk on Christmas Eve with a cut head he had sustained from a fall and Healy had carried him up to bed. His wound would have dropped blood onto Healy's clothes. The defence left it there; they had made their point.

It had been a busy schedule and the magistrates decided that enough had been heard for one day. They asked the prosecution how much more evidence they wished to produce and Sims told them that perhaps another half a dozen witnesses would be needed. The matter was adjourned until 18 March.

Chapter 23

The Country Grinds On

With a week's breathing space, the police officers had time to go over the facts again to make sure nothing had been missed. It was now thirty-five days since Wensley had first stepped into the small corner shop in Nightingale Road, and it was no more welcoming now than it had been then. The cold and snow had persisted and the house was only kept comfortable by the single fire in the upstairs front room. Information still trickled in, and Kirby was sent to see a local licensee who had been on the main road outside Hitchin on the morning Mrs Ridgley's body had been found. He had seen a man running towards Luton who loosely fitted the description of Healy. When shown the photograph of the man charged with the murder, the publican was merely able to say that 'he somewhat resembled the man he saw'.[98] Sightings like this were common, people wanting to help the police with information, but more often than not they weren't connected in any way, but they all needed following up. Attention to detail was important and nothing could be overlooked or taken to chance. Satisfied that everything that could be done was in hand, Wensley once again read the reports in the paper to make sure that the public were getting the best information.

He shivered with cold, wrapped his coat tighter around himself and flicked through the rest of the newspapers spread out on the table in front of him. He wrestled with the idea of chasing a war veteran for the murder of a helpless old woman and thought again about the state of the world after the war. The government was now promising to knock down slums and replace them with better housing, but soldiers still in the army were becoming restless. They wanted to go home, and more and more were getting drunk and ending up in fights, often going to prison, when only a few months earlier they were fighting the enemy in the fields of Flanders. Wensley looked out of the window and wondered where Healy sat in all this. Was he just a victim of the war struggling to make ends meet, possibly mentally disturbed by what he had witnessed on the battlefields, or was he simply a violent man who dismissed the life of others? After a few minutes, he shook his head as if something brought him back to reality and refocussed on the task in hand.

Chapter 24

Another Nail in the Coffin

A week later, the court resumed and the prosecution presented their last witnesses. The newspapers made much of the fact that Healy was a war veteran and had served at Mons during the war and had been awarded the 1914 Star, the British War Medal and the Victory Medal, but this wasn't a time for sentiment. In the statement, he made to the police, Healy had said that he had been drinking on the night in question in the Plough and Dial public house and had left sometime before closing time. In fact, he clarified, he probably would have been home by closing time, yet both Annie Smith and his wife had said he had come home at 10.30pm. Percy Gigg, the licensee of the public house was present to clarify the timings and what he knew about Healy. As he had said in his statement to the police, he confirmed that Healy was a regular drinker at his pub but was unable to recall whether he was there on Saturday, 25 January. Even if he was there, he said, closing time was 9pm and he wouldn't have been on the premises after that; the only other person who worked at the pub was his wife. Cross-examination by Passingham ably made the point that the public house was busy that evening and may account for the licensee's inability to recollect Healy being there that night. So, where was Healy between 9pm and 10.30pm if Smith, Gigg and Annie Healy were all correct in their accounts? Wensley knew what this amounted to. Healy didn't have an alibi.

Given the evidence presented by the defence the previous week about McCarton's claims to have bled on Healy, the prosecution decided to recall Mavis Smith. She was specifically questioned about the lodger and she said that McCarton had come into the house and sat in a chair. He had a bloodied head, but it was only a slight injury and was no longer bleeding and despite Healy offering to wash it for him, McCarton wouldn't let him. Despite this, Healy asked her mother to fetch some water as he obviously still intended to tend to his wound, and in order to do this, he removed his coat and rolled up his sleeves. When Annie Smith returned with the water, McCarton still refused for his wound to be washed and sat in the chair for half an hour before Healy helped him upstairs to his bed. The point had been made, Wensley hoped, that it was highly unlikely that any of McCarton's blood could have got onto Healy's sleeves as they were rolled up.

To drive home the prosecution's notion that Healy had been attacked by the dog, Dr Grellett was recalled and asked to describe what he had seen in the house and describe the injuries to the prisoner. Starting with the inside of the property, he stated that he examined the four-pound weight and saw, attached to it, a six-inch-long hair, which was probably human but other hairs stuck to it were brown and coarser and seemed to be dog hairs. When he examined the prisoner's hands, his opinion was that some injuries were recent but others were still healing with scabs on. These injuries were probably some weeks old and he thought it possible that they had bled profusely. Judging by the puncture wound on the thumb, the injuries could have been caused by a dog bite. He had also examined the rest of Healy's body and found a recent abrasion on the prisoner's shoulder. At this point, Tindall-Lucas asked if the prisoner could be brought forward so that the bench could more closely examine the injuries to the prisoner's hand for themselves. Healy was escorted forwarded and the magistrates, in turn, looked closely at his hands, inspecting the injuries, which were still clearly visible.

Sergeant Brewer was then summoned to the witness box and gave evidence about Healy's remuneration from the army, as he had now confirmed, as suggested by Annie Healy in her statement to the police, that on 31 January 1919, the week after the discovery of the body, he had received an army gratuity of £8.10s thus giving the reason, said the defence, why he was in possession of money and able to pay off his debts and buy himself some clothes. Brewer confirmed the possibility. He was then asked by the prosecutor to confirm the damage to the trousers he had taken from Healy. There were 'two recent rents' he said, and thinking his evidence was complete he prepared to leave the witness stand. But Passingham wanted to cross-examine further. Alluding to conversations that had been reported to him, the solicitor asked Brewer whether he had spoken to Healy's wife recently and because of complaints of her alleged objectionable behaviour to the witnesses in the house, he had suggested to her that she ought to seek fresh lodgings and that if she had nowhere to go, she should go to the workhouse. Brewer denied this, but it was a clear attempt to show that the police had adopted a jaundiced view towards Mrs Healy.

The khaki handkerchief issue had to be resolved, and Constable Kirby gave evidence that he had found three new khaki handkerchiefs in the glass cabinet in the living room at Nightingale Road and had compared these to the one tied around Mrs Ridgley's neck. In his opinion, he said, 'it was a different sort of handkerchief altogether'. Tindall-Lucas wanted to satisfy himself on this point and directed Kirby to bring the handkerchiefs to court. After a short break, Kirby returned and handed the items to the chairman of the bench who, with his colleagues, concluded that there was a marked difference in texture, hem and size. Wensley thought back to Reed's earlier conclusion that the shop was the source of the handkerchief. How wrong he had been. Negligence, incompetence or merely trying to avoid a difficult investigation in his last few months of service? He focussed back on the proceedings.

Despite Bernard Spilsbury saying he had found no blood on the broken file he had examined, Sims chose to clarify the context of the tool being found and Detective Constable Waters was recalled to explain how it had been discovered. He had searched the prisoner's bedroom upon his arrest, and in a suitcase under the bed he had found the broken file, which he seized, together with sheets from the prisoner's bed and a clay pipe. For the sake of completeness, he also mentioned that he searched a chest of drawers and found the waistband of a pair of pants and some sticking plaster. These additional items hadn't been handed to Spilsbury for examination but the file had. His early thoughts had been that this was a potential weapon, hence it being submitted for blood analysis.

Having clarified that point, he then told the court that he had walked from 16, Radcliffe Road to the Plough and Dial public house and it had taken him thirteen minutes walking at 3½ miles per hour; he had tested this using two different routes, one via Nightingale Road, the other via Queen Street. The implication was that if Healy had been in the public house that evening it was in relative close proximity to Mrs Ridgley's shop. Had he left well before closing time, if he was there at all, he had time to get to the shop and murder Ridgley. Having murdered her, he wasn't seen again by anyone until 10.30pm when he returned home.

With the majority of the evidence the prosecution wished to tender at this stage having been laid before the magistrates, Wensley then gave his evidence. He largely reiterated details of the arrest and how he had conducted the investigation having assumed responsibility for it on 6 February at the request of Chief Constable Law. Passingham seized upon the opportunity to challenge the man who was in charge and focussed on the integrity of the investigation. He pushed Wensley on whether, on 15 February, when Healy willingly went to the police station, he was under arrest. Wensley replied that he wasn't, as he had no evidence at that time with which to charge him. He had taken a statement from him and while at the police station he saw the injury to the prisoner's hand and subsequently asked the doctor to examine him.

Now referring specifically to the statement Healy had made, Passingham asked him why, on 18 February, at the prisoner's first appearance before the court when he, Wensley, had promised to furnish him with the statement, he had still failed to do so. Further, Passingham still hadn't been provided with the photographs and plan of the house, having to rely on those provided to the court and without the opportunity to study them beforehand. Wensley had no answer to this and Passingham turned to the magistrates exclaiming that the bench and the public should know how these cases were being conducted. He argued vociferously that Healy should have been cautioned prior to him making a statement. The atmosphere in the court darkened as Tindall-Lucas commented that 'an official note would be taken of Mr Passingham's objection'. As if embarrassed, Wensley passed Healy's statement to the court, which in turn was handed to Passingham.

The prosecution case concluded, Passingham addressed the bench. 'There is no possible evidence upon which the bench can send the prisoner for trial,' he submitted. Buoyed by Reed's first conclusion that this was an accidental death, he continued that it was for the bench to say whether the evidence confirmed the theory of murder.[99] There had, he said, been no evidence put before the court that there had been a quarrel, revenge or a robbery, and when Healy was found to be in possession of £6.3s when arrested, this was because Healy had received his army gratuity. Passingham then focussed on Craswell, pointing out that as he had been unable to say whether Healy was wearing an overcoat, hat or cap, he may well be mistaken in his identity. He pointed out, 'if he saw that man in the shop and took sufficient notice of him to know what he purchased, he ought to be able to tell you how that man was dressed.'

The defence solicitor submitted to the court that as Healy rarely smoked a pipe, why was it that, according to Craswell, he had bought tobacco from Mrs Ridgley? An examination of a pipe found in Healy's bedroom showed, in his submission, that very little tobacco had passed through it. Passingham gathered momentum as he picked away at the prosecution case. Despite the fact that whoever killed Mrs Ridgley must have come away with a great deal of blood on them, only a few spots of blood had been found on the prisoner's clothes and which may have been caused by injuries to the prisoner's hand. He pointed out that there had been some confusion as to the time Healy arrived back at the house on the Saturday night because of the clock being fast. In any event, Smith, he argued, didn't notice anything unusual or strange about the prisoner or his clothes when he came back. Had Healy murdered Ridgley he would have been covered in blood and that would have been noticed even if he was only in the room for half a minute, and he pointed out that Healy had only one suit. It couldn't be agreed between the Smiths, he continued, what time Healy had come downstairs the following day, and whatever the cause of Healy's injuries to his hand, which Passingham submitted was only a scratch, this hadn't caused him to stay off work, hence the reason why he hadn't found the need to report the injury to his employers. Finally, he maintained that while Healy's statement was correct in every way, it shouldn't be allowed to be submitted in evidence for reasons he had already outlined.

After one hour and fifty minutes, Passingham sat down and the magistrates retired to consider the evidence. Fifteen minutes later, they returned and Tindall-Lucas announced, 'The bench decides that there is a case to answer.' Asked if he had anything to say, Healy said no, pleaded not guilty and chose to reserve his defence. At 4.30pm, Healy was committed in custody for trial at Hertfordshire Assizes and Wensley and Law retired, relieved and pleased that the matter would appear before a jury. Something had been salvaged from the calamitous past and Chief Constable Law returned to his office and penned a letter to the commissioner of the Metropolitan Police:

> 'Sir,
>
> 'I desire to bring to your notice the extremely able and tactful manner in which Chief Inspector Wensley and his assistants have conducted this enquiry, with the result that John Healy has been committed for Trial at the next Hertfordshire Assizes on the capital charge.
>
> 'The circumstances connected with this case were unusual in that the local Superintendent of Police had formed a definite theory of accidental death prior to my application to you for expert assistance, consequently the case required considerable tact and perspicacity in order to bring it to a successful issue and to avoid friction with local officers.

'I am glad to say that Chief Inspector Wensley has carried out his investigation to my entire satisfaction and that his efforts are appreciated by myself and all officers of this force with whom he came in contact.

'I shall be grateful if you would kindly cause him to be so informed.

I am,

Sir,

Your obedient Servant.'[100]

Back in his office at Scotland Yard, Wensley was less sanguine. There were too many loose ends, and he knew he could do next to nothing to tie them up. But he still held out for that gem which could help the case once and for all; the location where the ration book was found. He sought approval for a financial reward and the *Hertfordshire Express* went to print on 22 March with a public notice:

A £1 reward will be paid to any person giving information that will lead to the IDENTITY OF THE GIRLS who found at Hitchin towards the end of January a RATION CARD BOOK in the name of JOHN HEALY, giving the address of 3, Ickleford Road and who took the same to 3, Ickleford Road and finally to the Hitchin Food Control Office. Information should be given by letter to CHIEF INSPECTOR WENSLEY, NEW SCOTLAND YARD.

He now put pen to paper to keep his senior officers apprised, summarised the latest developments but then decided to add a salutary note to its conclusion:

'I have no hesitation in saying that had our aid been invoked earlier we should have been able to have presented an even stronger case against the prisoner than we have.'[101]

He submitted his report and went home. He needed a rest.

Chapter 25

The Prosecution

Hertfordshire Assizes started its summer session at the Shire Hall, Hertford on Monday, 16 June 1919, with the presiding judge, Mr Justice Darling, overseeing the list of cases now brought before him. Darling had been appointed to the bench in 1897, had presided over many criminal trials and had developed a reputation for making unhelpful comedic quips during proceedings, a practice which attracted criticism in the press. It was a busy list and the judge peered at it over his glasses: a young woman charged with housebreaking and theft; an eighteen-year-old man accused of a series of indecent assaults; another accused of cutting the throat of his daughter and then trying to kill himself; and cases of bigamy, frauds and bankruptcy. Number two on his list was John Healy (33), labourer, murder of an old woman at Hitchin. He didn't particularly stand out; there were other murders to deal with and some of the other defendants were, like Healy, either serving or former soldiers during the war. Darling spent the Monday dealing with the majority of the cases as guilty pleas were entered and merely had to deal with mitigation and sentencing. Healy, however, pleaded not guilty, 'Puts' – a shorthand term meaning that the accused 'puts' himself on offer to his fellow citizens to try him – was entered in the court record and the case was adjourned to the following day.

On Tuesday, Healy was formally charged with the murder of Mrs Ridgley. The prosecution was to be conducted by Sir Edward Marshall Hall KC and Mr Adrian Clark, and representing the defendant was Mr Cecil Hayes and Mr F.G.L. Bridgeman.

Though Marshall Hall had built up a reputation as one of the great defence barristers, on this occasion he was prosecuting and Wensley knew that despite his understanding of the complexities of cases, his weakness was in fact that he lacked skill at arguing points of law and was entirely unembarrassed by this fundamental flaw. He wasn't a great lawyer, nor even a very good one, and once turned to his junior in court saying, 'You must take this point, there's some law in it'. Wensley knew that as an advocate he favoured the theatrical manner, was emotional, often bordering on hysterical, and somewhat apt to overstate the case. His judgements were not always sound and he was disposed to be swayed by his likes and dislikes. Equally, he wasn't a well man. Some years earlier he had almost died due to double pneumonia, and the varicose veins which now troubled him necessitated wearing bandages from foot to groin to alleviate the pain as well as needing a nasal spray to deal with his catarrh.

Wensley watched nervously as the jury were sworn in. The original senior officer, Superintendent Reed, had now retired and it would be Wensley who would be expected to answer questions on the conduct of the investigation. He wasn't expecting an easy trial and he brooded a little. Despite all his efforts and notices in newspapers, he had failed to find the 'ration book children', something he still maintained would add considerable weight to the case. But it wasn't to be, and now the packed courthouse fell silent watching each of the jurors [102] take the oath and glance repeatedly at Healy as he stood in the dock. This was probably going to be the most remarkable trial with which the town of Hitchin was ever likely to be associated. Once the jury had been fully sworn, Marshall Hall stood up to address the twelve men in his opening speech, journalists with their pens poised and members of the public leaning forward hoping to hear every word above the noise of children playing outside whose laughter and voices flowed through the open courthouse windows. It was a very hot summer day. He opened with an emphatic plea, knowing that the case had excited great interest, telling the jury about the need to ensure that they must disregard anything they have thought of or heard about. He paused and then began outlining the prosecution case.

He described the finding of the body of Mrs Ridgley and her dog, that she had been murdered and that she had no bank account. Typically, he said, she would take somewhere between £10 and £12 a day on a Saturday and then told them that they would hear evidence from George Rutland, who, on the night in question, saw her front door open and a light shining from her shop window at an hour which was later than would be normal and thereby singular. A short while later, the shop door was closed. He then turned his address to the evidence of the Roach family and how they had heard noises consistent with the shopkeeper and her dog being attacked before her dead body was eventually found by the police on the Monday morning. He described the inside of the shop, where the bodies were found and the extent of each of their injuries, emphasising the apron, and the khaki handkerchief wrapped around the deceased's neck. There had been a great deal of blood, he said, and described the four-pound weight which had been found close to the bodies. Hall adjusted his demeanour slightly, less dramatic than he had been hitherto, and explained how there had been an inquest and the body had been buried without a post mortem. Only once the chief constable had returned and been notified, had the services of Scotland Yard been invoked.

At this point, the judge, who had already read the case papers relating to the trial, asked a question, and he had clearly had been waiting for this moment. 'On what theory did the coroner's jury find a verdict of accidental death?'

Marshall Hall replied, 'It was the theory of a police superintendent, since retired, but I am at a loss to know how any theory of accidental death could have prevailed in the mind of anybody who had had any experience in such matters.'

Darling continued his interjection. 'I was astounded to hear that anybody could come to the conclusion that the woman was killed by falling amongst pots and pans as was then suggested.'

'Nor I, because it has been proved beyond all reasonable doubt that this woman was murdered,' Marshall Hall responded.

As if to take the heat out of the situation, Cecil Hayes rose to address the judge and said of the accidental death conclusion, 'This is not my theory at all. I agree with what your Lordship says.'

Darling looked about the court, as if he had satisfactorily made his point, and nodded for the prosecution to continue. Marshall Hall picked up from where he had been in his speech when he was interrupted and eased back into barrister's rhetoric describing the proximity of Healy's house to the corner shop. He summarised how the Smith family and a man called Christiansen, with whom Healy lived, would describe the events of the evening of Saturday, 25 January, and how the Irish labourer had come home late that night, having earlier been seen hanging around outside the shop. He told the jurors of the injuries to the prisoner's finger seen the next day and how his statement, which he made to the police, had stated where he had been that night and how he had, according to him, suffered the injury to his hand. Finishing with the injured finger, he said a doctor would be called to say that the injuries were consistent with a dog bite.

With gusto, Marshall Hall continued. Evidence would be introduced to show that after the murder of Mrs Ridgley, Healy had bloodstained clothing, had bought new clothes, and despite his denials that he had been in the shop in recent times, a witness would be called to contradict that.

Turning his attention to the defendant, he made it clear that establishing his whereabouts at the time of the murder was vital and held up the statement made by Healy on the night he was arrested and which gave his account of the circumstances. There were three crucial aspects to this case, he said, and what Healy told the police on the night he was arrested must be taken into account. There was no objection from the defence to Marshall Hall introducing the statement in evidence, despite Passingham's protestations at the remand hearings that it should be inadmissible. He then itemised the three aspects contained in the prisoner's statement which he said were the important factors. Firstly, the injuries to his thumb and finger were a result of an accident at work two weeks before he was arrested and therefore after the night of the murder; he could disprove that. Secondly, he had not bought any new clothes since the murder; he could disprove that. Thirdly, he had not been in Mrs Ridgley's shop in recent months; he could disprove that.

He then offered his theory on the murder. The murderer, he said, secreted himself in the deceased's house, she found him, there was an altercation, the dog interfered and the man seized the weight and bashed the woman on the head after dealing with the dog. He paused to allow the information to be absorbed and then concluded by describing the downstairs as 'a confusion' while upstairs had not been interfered with, despite there being a large amount of money there. The murderer, Marshall Hall opined, made his escape through the back door and garden. He now looked sternly at the jury and gathered his thoughts before delivering his next line. 'It was a serious matter,' he said, 'especially for people in rural districts, if a woman is to be done in this way without any discovery of the person responsible.' He gave time for this last comment to sink in, but, satisfied that his opening speech had been successfully delivered, he called his first witness. The jury and gathered spectators sat back to hear the details. Wensley relaxed a little.

One by one, fifteen witnesses[103] stood in the witness box and told their part of the story, repeating only what they had previously said at either the inquest or the series of remand hearings leading to Healy's committal for trial. Each was closely cross-examined by Cecil Hayes, who carefully suggested that witnesses who spoke specifically about Healy were in some way wrong in their recollections, especially the Smiths about injuries to his hand, and he even got Mavis Smith to acknowledge that when Healy had paid off his rent arrears on 31 January, that it was possible that he had acquired that money by virtue of an army gratuity which had been due to him.

Mr Justice Darling, renowned for his jocular interventions, couldn't resist such an opportunity when the landlady's daughter was speaking about the evening of Sunday 26 January, the night after the murder. Marshall Hall had asked Smith whether she had noticed Healy's condition that evening and she had replied, 'Yes, he was drunk.'

Hayes immediately sprang to his feet and objected. 'How can this witness say whether the man was drunk or not?'

Darling retorted, 'It is generally very simple to tell whether a man is drunk or not. It depends on how drunk.'

The courtroom burst into laughter.

Healy had not given evidence at the earlier inquest or the magistrates' hearings and he casually followed the proceedings almost with a spectator's interest. He never appeared listless, nor excited. As counsel spoke, on a number of occasions, his open and rather attractive features suggested a degree of amused interest in what was going on; his face indicated rather more than a shadow of a smile as his eyes moved from witness to judge and from judge to jury, never affording a glance at the public crowd.

When William Craswell stepped into the witness box, the prosecution knew his evidence was crucial, but providing he said what he had said in his evidence at the remand hearing, then everything would be satisfactory. Examined by Marshall Hall, he again told the story of seeing Healy in the shop on the night in question and how he had bought some tobacco and matches; he had recognised his picture in the newspaper, he said. Marshall Hall sat down and Hayes rose. He chose his questions carefully.

'Did you look closely at the man who came into the shop while you were there?' he asked.

'I did not take any particular notice of him.'

'You took so little particular notice that you are unable to say whether the man had a hat or cap on?'

'I could not tell you,' replied Craswell.

Hayes then adjusted his voice and pointedly asked the witness why he hadn't given evidence at the inquest of Mrs Ridgley on 19 February yet was able to do so on 4 March at the remand hearing. Wensley, sitting at the back of the court, expected this question but knew that Brewer had asked Craswell specifically about this when he returned to see him and he remembered that his response had been that he had since seen Healy's photo in the *Daily Sketch*. He had already said this in his evidence. What he hadn't said was that he subsequently thought he *had* imparted the information to the police but in fact he had told someone who in truth was a journalist.

It was a credible story and the detective sat waiting for Craswell to say the same again.

But Craswell said something completely different. Referring to when he was first spoken to by the police, he said, 'I tried to make a doubt about seeing him in case I should be called to try and pick him.'

Hayes said nothing. He wanted a period of silence for the impact of what had just been said to sink into the minds of the jury. Craswell had been disingenuous. He didn't want to get involved. He was a weak link in the prosecution case.

This wasn't what Wensley expected to hear, but Hayes did. He had clearly done his homework, for he pushed Craswell and asked him specifically that when he first spoke to the police in the person of Sergeant Gravestock whether he had said that when he was in the shop that night there was no one else in there? Craswell adamantly denied the accusation, and in such a way that Hayes seemed to have lost his advantage. However, he had cast doubt on the integrity of the witness, and knowing that, he sat down, pleased with himself, and waited for the next witness.

It was Dr Grellett, and when cross-examined by Hayes he said only that it was *probable* that the weight had caused the injuries to the deceased and that the injuries to the prisoner's hand, while consistent with a dog bite, 'may equally have been caused in some other way'.

The court's atmosphere was electric as Hayes chipped away at the prosecution case but was temporarily interrupted during the examination of the next witness, Mrs Chandler. In an attempt to determine the source of the bloodstained handkerchief, the witness was handed the exhibit which had been removed from her sister's neck, and as it was passed to her, Marshall Hall explained to the court that due to an accident at the inquest, the garment had unfortunately become ink-stained. Justice Darling took the opportunity.

'Every precaution seems to have been taken in the early days to ensure that nobody should be detected,' he barked out.

More laughter echoed throughout the court before solemnity returned.

Constable Kirby again gave his evidence about the discovery of the body and what he had seen inside the house. When he was passed the bloodstained cigar box which had been used as a till and the bloodstained cardboard jam canister, keen to understand the lack of fingerprint evidence, his Lordship asked the officer if he too could inspect them. The items were passed to the judge who, squinting his eyes, examined them very closely and after a few seconds asked whether it had been observed that there were marks of a bloody finger or thumb upon the cigar box.

'Yes,' said prosecuting counsel, 'but they are of no value as the box had been handled by so many.'

Turning specifically to Kirby and holding up the canister, the judge asked, 'Did you notice the two finger-marks on this canister?'

'Yes.'

'Did Superintendent Reed see them?' the judge persisted.

'He handled the canister,' Kirby recalled.

'It was perfectly obvious that somebody with bloody fingers had handled it?'

'Yes.'

Accepting Kirby's answers but with an obvious air of annoyance, he commented that it was only fair to say that the marks were so indistinct that the ordinary fingerprint test would have been worthless. This dramatic intervention by the judge was heightened as the prosecution produced an unrolled piece of linoleum which had covered the counter in the shop and which showed blood marks upon it. The jury looked on, as if perfectly understanding the judge's line of questioning.

It was now Warren's turn, and having replaced Reed as superintendent since his retirement the month before, he was closely questioned on the conduct of the investigation. Reed, he said, had the case to himself, had no one supervising him and had no detective experience and didn't seek to employ one. He confirmed that he himself had helped search the house, and when asked specifically about any fingerprints, he limply explained that no bloodstained fingerprints that were good enough for photographing were found as 'it was very dark and a lot of people had been walking about since the murder'. He emphasised that Reed searched the house the previous evening without the aid of a torch, using only a magnifying glass and a candle. He told the court that, at the time, the chief constable was away, but as soon as he returned he at once asked for the services of Scotland Yard. The judge listened intently to these excuses and at one point turned to the jury and sarcastically commented that 'so far as we can see, only the police thought the dog was killed by Mrs Ridgley'.

With tempers rising, after a full day, at five o'clock the court adjourned until the following morning, but with the police not being portrayed in a good light, a distinct feeling existed in the building that an acquittal might follow. Newspaper reporters whispered, and the public mumbled their own theories.

Tomorrow, the jury would reach its verdict and Wensley's concerns were deepening.

Chapter 26

The Defence

When the case resumed at ten thirty the next morning, Wensley spoke about the conduct of the investigation after he had assumed responsibility on 6 February. During the course of this evidence, the detective made a specific point of commending Constable Kirby for the work he had carried out on the investigation. Wensley saw this as a way of thanking Kirby for his continued hard work after having to supress his earlier frustrations when seeing an obvious murder being dismissed by his superintendent as an accident. Hayes' only line of cross-examination was in connection with the statement that his client had made to the police on 15 February and suggested to him that the officer had put 'leading' or 'guiding' questions to him in order to elicit his account. Wensley declined to accept counsel's suggestion.

Following Wensley was Dr Bernard Spilsbury, and the public gasped out loud as he made his way through the court, immaculately dressed, carrying a briefcase in one hand and a skull in the other. As he stepped into the witness box, he carefully placed the object of morbid attention on the handrail. The judge, equally surprised, but aware of Spilsbury's idiosyncrasies, looked at the witness and nodded towards the body part now on open display. Understanding the judge's gesture, the pathologist nonchalantly clarified that he intended to use the skull to assist the jury in understanding the nature of the injuries, but no, it wasn't that of the victim, Mrs Ridgley. The expressions of relief could be heard around the court; wry smiles appeared on the faces of counsel.

The drama of his entrance having subsided, the business of his evidence began. He outlined the findings of the post mortem he had conducted on the deceased, lifting the skull up on occasions to show the judge and jury where injuries had been sustained, his interpretation of the scene and his opinion of the injuries and markings on the prisoner's clothing. At one point, Spilsbury ventured that, having examined the bloodstaining on the garments, it seemed that the two shirts which had been taken from the prisoner appeared to have been worn one on top of the other. Mrs Ridgley had been murdered, he said, and possibly with the four-pound weight which had been found at the scene; the victim's injuries were consistent with this. The bloodstaining and injuries to the defendant's hand were consistent with what might reasonably be expected to be found on someone who had carried out the attack, including the probability of injuries consistent with dog bites. Cross-examination by Hayes elicited only one real issue in that Spilsbury agreed that to determine the exact age of the bloodstains on the prisoner's clothing was impossible. With his evidence concluded, the prosecution closed their case; it was now time for the defence.

Hayes called only three witnesses. The first two, Thomas Cain and Richard Reeves, were employees at Kryn and Lahy who had worked with the prisoner and who both stated that they never saw Healy wearing a bandage. Having established doubt as to whether Healy had an injury to his hand in the days after the murder, Hayes called his client to the witness box and the hushed audience watched as he slowly made his way from the dock. The decision to call the prisoner as a witness was a big one, and Hayes had considered the pros and cons of calling Healy. Until 1898, the law did not allow for prisoners to speak in court, and any evidence they wished to give had to be voiced through their counsel. The law had now changed and a person charged with a criminal offence had the opportunity to give their side of the story. But it was a double-edged sword. On the one hand, it showed to a jury the character and demeanour of the prisoner in the dock and provided the opportunity for a prisoner to convince a court of their innocence and perhaps explain matters in a way in which counsel wrestled. Equally, defence counsel would readily point out to a jury that the prisoner was under no obligation whatsoever to give evidence and therefore by doing so would show that he has nothing to hide. On the other hand, it exposed the defendant to the often hostile cross-examination of prosecution counsel, and traditionally, since the act had been passed, they had made poor witnesses, often blurting out comments that undermined the defence case. Hayes knew that Marshall Hall had the power to almost petrify a witness, let alone the defendant, who was under extreme pressure in capital cases to save himself from the gallows. He also knew Mr Justice Darling's attitude towards prisoners who gave their own evidence, remembering the Seddon murder trial in 1912 when Darling sat as one of the appeal judges. 'No one who is well acquainted with criminal administration,' he had said, 'is ignorant of the fact today, prisoners are practically bound to go into the box and that in the great majority of cases, they say what is not true.' Hayes also knew that Marshall Hall had successfully defended the first man to take advantage of this new piece of legislation. He would now be relishing the opportunity to cross-examine Healy.

Healy seemed passive, almost indifferent as he stood up straight, as if to attention, facing the court ready for the first question. He was led by Hayes in teasing out his background and he spoke clearly as he outlined the details of his army service, his marriage and his arrival in Hitchin.

He was asked by his barrister to tell the court about his life in Hitchin and to account for his movements on Saturday, 25 January. Healy told judge and jury that he had moved to 16, Radcliffe Road in November and had been employed as a labourer ever since, earning good money. On the day of the tragedy, he had walked in the morning to Letchworth, returning home about 6pm. He had supper and went to the Plough and Dial public house, remaining there until about closing time, which was confirmed and accepted by the court as 9pm. He then walked into town, specifically Market Square, and had walked along Nightingale Road and then walked back along Station Road and Hermitage Road.. When asked, he said he arrived home around 9pm or just before, read the paper for a while, spoke to some of the other tenants and retired to bed about 10.30pm. He denied having any injury to his finger the next day, and in fact had incurred the injury at work on 28 January and had never visited Mrs Ridgley's shop since he had been living at Radcliffe Road.

Marshall Hall stood up to cross-examine him. 'According to your story, you got home at nine o'clock. What did you do between seven and nine?'

'I was in that public house.'

'From seven to nine?'

'I don't mean to say I was inside that house from seven to nine.'

'Well, how long do you say you were there?'

'I might be there for an hour.'

'That is from seven to eight. What did you do between eight and nine?'

'I got out in the street and walked around the Market Square, where I generally walked.'

Marshall Hall moved on to the next stage. 'How long do you say you stayed in the kitchen reading and talking?'

'At least twenty minutes – in the dining hall.'

'Who was there?'

'Mrs Smith, Miss Smith, Bernard Smith and my wife.'

'You say you were in bed by half past ten. If you got home at nine and stayed twenty minutes in the dining hall, what did you do in the intervening time?'

'I sat reading the paper.'

'Where?'

'In the dining hall.'

'Then you were there more than twenty minutes. How long did it take you to get into bed?'

'A couple of minutes.'

Marshall Hall persisted. 'What did you do between nine and half past ten?'

'I cannot say how long I was in the dining hall. It might be twenty minutes.'

Summarising, Marshall Hall commented, 'That leaves nearly an hour unaccounted for. What were you doing in that hour?'

'I am only roughly guessing the time I went in.'

Marshall Hall made his move. 'I suggest you did not get home till half past ten, and you went straight to bed.'

'That is not true.'

'Were you in the neighbourhood of Nightingale Road that evening?'

'No, sir.'

Prosecution counsel continued to probe around the timings and location of his movements and he reminded Healy of the evidence of Mavis Smith and Christiansen. Both, Healy said, were mistaken.

Marshall Hall then handed him Annie Healy's statement that she had made to the police and asked him to confirm that it was her signature on the document, though it was signed with just an 'X'. He said it was.

'If your wife says you came home about ten o'clock, would that be right?'

'No, sir.'

'Did your wife tear a piece off her camisole and bind up your finger for you on the Sunday morning?'

'No, sir,' and he added that this had been done on the following Sunday, 2 February.

Marshall Hall then turned to the evidence of William Craswell, who the day before had said about seeing Healy in the shop buying tobacco.

'Do you say he has invented it or made a mistake?'

His response resonated throughout the courtroom.

'Either Craswell or me is telling lies, and may Almighty God strike the liar dead.'[104]

The courtroom exploded in sensation, the public barely able to believe their ears. Equally shocked, Mr Justice Darling stepped in.

'No, no, you must not talk like that.'

Marshall Hall seized the moment. Healy was agitated.

'Don't get excited. I am to suggest to you,' the King's Counsel said, 'that you are a most excitable person and get into a very violent temper on the smallest provocation.'

'I think I might be at hearing all the evidence against me.'

'Have you had trouble with your brother, Tom? Do you remember when you were struck over the head with the tongs to keep you quiet?'

'Yes,' replied the prisoner, 'but it was his temper that caused the trouble on that occasion.'

Prosecution counsel drove his point home. 'I suggest that when you get excited you don't know what you do.'

Healy replied, 'No.'

Noticing that Marshall Hall had paused for thought, the judge asked a question. 'Did you hear Craswell say that he had no doubt you were the man he saw in Mrs Ridgley's shop on the Saturday night when she was killed?'

'Yes, but I was never in that shop on that night.'

The question had given Marshall Hall time to think, and he continued with his line of cross-examination. 'How do you account for the blood on those two shirts of yours?'

'I don't know.'

'Can you give me any explanation?'

'No, unless I cut my face when I was shaving.'

'Do you wipe your face with the front part or the tail of your shirt?'

'If I was shaving and my shirt was hanging down I should.'

Healy thought for a while and then told the court that he would routinely wear the two shirts on top of one another. The judge looked up, and remembering Dr Spilsbury's evidence where he had suggested just such a possibility, he expressed the view that this reasoning by Spilsbury had been remarkable and said it was an instance of the value of circumstantial evidence.

Now turning specifically to the wounded finger, and in answer to a question, Healy said that he had never had a puncture wound to his finger. The judge, seeing this as an important aspect of the case, asked, 'Do you deliberately swear that?'

'I do, My Lord.'

Having got this assurance, Darling directed that both Spilsbury and Grellett approach the prisoner to point out the wound to the prisoner's thumb, and there was a sense of subdued excitement as the two medical men approached the witness box. Both doctors agreed that the wound was no longer visible but that there was a curved nodule, deep in the skin, which could be felt and was on the site of the puncture wound Grellett had previously witnessed. Directed by the judge, Healy was paraded in front of each member of the jury and the judge himself, allowing them to examine the finger in turn. Despite this graphical and invasive presentation of evidence, Healy maintained that he never had a puncture wound, and when Grellett had examined him on 17 February, although having scratches over his hand, he didn't have a wound as described by the police surgeon.

Healy had been in the witness box for nearly an hour when he was handed the four-pound weight. Answering a specific question, Healy said he had never seen it before and Marshall Hall told Healy to hold the weight as if he was attacking a dog. Without hesitation, the prisoner held it up, at the same time telling the court that if he were to use such a method against a ferocious dog, he would have thrown it at the animal.

Marshall Hall was nearing completion and posed a final question to Healy, asking him why, according to him, all the witnesses were lying? Healy replied that he felt the Smiths in particular had a grudge due to a dispute they'd had with him involving money last Christmas.

'They wanted to banish me from the town of Hitchin,' he declared.

'Do you suggest that Mrs Smith and her daughter and son have invented their evidence against you in order to get you convicted? Do you really mean that?' Marshall Hall enquired.

'It's to get me away from the town of Hitchin at any rate.'

Marshall Hall sat down and Hayes rose to tell the man trying to save his own life he had no further questions for him. He was escorted back to the dock. As the prisoner attracted excited eyes from the public gallery, Wensley reflected on what he had just heard. Healy had never given the impression of being confused. Other than his one outburst, he had answered questions in cross-examination readily and freely, indifferent to and seemingly unconscious of any inconsistencies. He had done what he wanted to do.

Defence counsel called no other witnesses. The prosecution team knew that the prisoner's wife's statement undermined much of what he had said on oath but were equally aware that she couldn't be compelled to give evidence against her husband, albeit Marshall Hall had, surprisingly, been allowed to refer to its contents. If she had given evidence, she would have had to deal with matters such as the time he came home that night, the cut finger and his ownership of khaki handkerchiefs, and in a way which didn't cast doubt on her husband's account. If it had suited the defence, Hayes could have called her as a witness, but the defence barristers knew that if she was called to give evidence, she could have been cross-examined by Marshall Hall. With that in mind, now that Healy had given his evidence, Hayes declared that the case for the defence had closed. He knew that he had to prove nothing and the onus was on the prosecution to prove the charge beyond all reasonable doubt.

Counsel's closing speeches took considerable time, both sides summarising their respective arguments and pointing out their opponent's weaknesses. Marshall Hall emphasised that the value of the evidence of the prosecution witnesses could hardly be in doubt and highlighted that he hadn't been given the opportunity to test Annie Healy's evidence, which doubtlessly would have supported the prosecution case. Privately though, he was exercised by the aggressive nature of Healy and was cognisant of the potential underlying reasons. The First World War had brought about fundamental changes in human behaviour. Being exposed to the traumas of trench warfare had led returning soldiers to commit crimes which beforehand they would never have committed, their behaviour brutalised by the casual regard to life. To them, life had become almost valueless. Medical staff particularly, such as Healy in the Royal Army Medical Corps, were pitched into a sickening, wearying nightmare round of clearing up in the wake of an unending trail of carnage. They had become unafraid of battle, murder and sudden death. Even Judge Darling had recently publicly announced that he felt that 'the harm that the war had done was far beyond any material damage that had been caused.' A correspondent had once written to Marshall Hall about this very point, arguing that it cannot be correct that men who had never been to war could be competent to try a man who had seen so much death that the matter was no longer of any importance. How were they able to understand the thinking and reasoning of such an individual when they had never seen such extreme violence themselves? The jury, the correspondent had argued, should be composed of men who had been in the trenches and would be aware of all the horror and how this can affect some men. Marshall Hall understood this, but the defence in this case was one of mistaken identity and lying witnesses, not one of insanity. Insanity was clearly established in law as a result of the McNaughton case in 1843, whereby a man could not be punished for an act unless he performed it with a guilty mind. If he carried out an act in a state of unconsciousness or complete madness, he cannot be said to have a 'guilty mind'. 'Unless a man is so mad as to be unable to appreciate the nature and quality of his act, or, alternatively, unable to distinguish right from wrong, he is responsible for all breaches of the law which he may commit.' However, unlike the general principle in law that the onus is on the prosecution to prove a case, in the case of insanity, the onus switches to the defence to prove that such insanity exists.

Marshall Hall wondered whether, had he been defending, he would have opted for this line of defence, particularly given the existence of insanity in Healy's family and that his mother had died in a lunatic asylum. But counsel had to work on the instructions given to him by the prisoner and he cannot construct a defence which he feels is more likely to succeed. Healy had nailed his colours to the mast; he wasn't mad – merely the police had got the wrong man.

Hayes, after outlining how important witnesses were mistaken or simply lying, made a special point of highlighting that the absence of bloodstains on the outer clothing of the prisoner made it virtually impossible for him to have committed the murder and in the process not get heavily bloodstained. Both barristers itemised each point methodically and, having completed their speeches, sat down to hear Mr Justice Darling address the jury and sum up the case. Darling pointed out in great detail the strong evidence against the accused, repeating that his wife, who could offer important evidence, had not been called by the defence. As if to reinforce his point from the day before, he told the jury that they should not conclude that the deceased had died as a result of an accident and, he emphasised, not even the defence associated themselves with the accident theory that somehow Mrs Ridgley had stumbled across pots and pans.

'It was the worst possible way,' he said, 'for a police officer to make up his mind as to the way in which a case had happened and then seek for evidence to bear out his view of the case.'

He continued by highlighting that as far as the prisoner was concerned, all the points put to him simply resulted in a denial. Could the jury have any doubts about who was telling the truth? Satisfied that he had covered the important points, he now looked at the jury and voiced his final direction.

'It is not a case where anyone saw the blows being struck. The evidence against the prisoner is made up of many small circumstances, and it is for you to say, whether so conclusively point in the one direction. – in the direction of his guilt – as to satisfy you that he is the man who murdered Mrs Ridgley. If you have a doubt about it, a reasonable doubt, such as you have in other affairs in life, you will say that he is not guilty. The prisoner is entitled to the benefit of any doubt you might have in your minds and in English law there is no verdict of 'Not Proven' and it does not follow that because a verdict of 'Not Guilty' is returned it necessarily follows that the prisoner was innocent but merely that his guilt has not been established to your satisfaction beyond any reasonable doubt. On the other hand, if you are satisfied beyond all reasonable doubt that he is the man, then you will find him guilty.'[105]

With these words ringing in their ears, the jury were led out of the court to consider their verdict. The time was 8.30pm.

Wensley had listened to the evidence intently and was largely satisfied with the way the trial had been conducted. He had not been surprised by the manner of the defence and other than Craswell giving an odd reason for his reticence in coming forward, all prosecution witnesses had come up to their statements. It had not been the strongest of prosecutions but he had been successful with weaker cases; he once again reflected on what could have been. A conviction, of course, would result in the hanging of Healy, and although he had previously seen the death sentence handed down by Mr Justice Hawkins four times in one week, he was not a fervent believer in capital punishment, recognising that there are many different reasons why people commit murder. He was considering this point when court officials, members of the public and journalists, who had barely had time to reflect on the day's proceedings, were interrupted by the jury indicating they had reached a verdict. The time was 8.42pm – just twelve minutes since they'd retired.

Surprised by the speed of matters, the court reconvened and the twelve men were brought back to the jury box. They were asked by the clerk of the court whether they had reached a verdict upon which they were all agreed; the foreman said they had.

'Is the defendant guilty or not guilty on the charge of the murder of Mrs Elizabeth Ridgley?'

The reply came in a silent courtroom. 'Not guilty.'

'And is that the verdict of you all?'

'It is.'

The judge turned to Healy and told him he was discharged. Almost dispassionately, he walked from the dock, shook hands with his counsel and then embraced his wife, who had sat silently for two days at the back of the court. As he left the building there was 'a tremendous crowd who showed unmistakable sympathy with the acquitted man and his wife. Throughout the trial, other than his one outburst, Healy had remained unperturbed and the newspapers described him as someone who 'must be a man of iron nerves.' Inside the court, the judge once more addressed the jury by thanking them for their work and exempted them from further jury service for five years.

Chapter 27

After the Trial

The world kept moving on. On the day that Healy was acquitted, the IRA was increasing its violence with the assassination of more policemen amidst allegations that the constabulary were using bayonets on civilians to enforce the law. And in the leafy streets of Epsom in Surrey, a police sergeant was killed as four hundred drunken Canadian soldiers stormed the police station to rescue two of their own who had been arrested for causing a disturbance. Fifteen police officers had been violently overwhelmed in their defence of the building. In his office in central London, the Director of Public Prosecutions, himself an experienced and successful barrister with huge influence, drafted out his letter to be typed. He had thought long and hard about its content before he signed and posted it to Scotland Yard.

'Sir,
'REX –v– HEALY
'ALLEGED MURDER – HERTFORD ASSIZES
'I cannot allow this case to be closed without an expression of commendation and even an admiration of the skilful work which was done in it by Chief Inspector Wensley and the Scotland Yard officers who were employed under him in the belated investigation which they were called in to make. To the Chief Inspector, it seems to me that the greatest credit is due for the collection of evidence of sufficient strength on which to have placed the accused upon his trial after the local constabulary had made so unaccountable a blunder as to attribute the death of the deceased to accident and not to design, and after the case had been presented to the Coroner and dealt with by the Coroner's Jury upon such an unreasonable hypothesis. The task presented to Scotland Yard, chiefly owing to is late presentment, was one of great difficulty, and one the execution

of which, if I may venture to say so, reflected the great credit upon Chief Inspector Wensley and his subordinates.

'I am, Sir,

Your obedient servant,

Charles W Mathews'[106]

Three days later, Wensley sat in his office in Scotland Yard writing *his* report.[107] He outlined the key points which he hoped would try and place some context around what he perceived as a 'failed investigation' and the first murder he had been involved with which had not resulted in a conviction. Without trying to attribute blame in any area, he pointed out that Sir Edward Marshall Hall had been appointed to the case only a few days before the trial, but that he, quickly understanding the central points of the prosecution asked whether more could be done to trace the girls who had found the ration book. Wensley argued that it couldn't have been progressed any further and reported that local rumour was that the parents were purposely keeping their children quiet. He believed that the book was found in the grounds of St Saviour's School, on the route between Mrs Ridgley' shop and Healy's house in Radcliffe Road but couldn't prove this.[108]

Referring to the prosecution witnesses, and despite Craswell's surprising comments in the witness box, he felt they all 'gave their evidence in a most creditable manner and came up to their statements in every detail. The statement taken by me from the prisoner on the night of 15th February 1919 was admitted in evidence without any protest from the defence'. He summarised the evidence given by each witness and concluded by saying that, effectively, the trial was the word of a large number of witnesses against that of Healy, who simply claimed that everyone was lying to get him ousted from Hitchin, where he wasn't welcome.

Wensley's final comments, however, were what he considered the real reason for the acquittal. He accepted that the word of a jury is final and that every man is innocent unless proven guilty, but he highlighted what he considered to be the most influential factors. The trial judge had been highly critical of Superintendent Reed's theory and his efforts to get evidence to support it and told the jury that it was the duty of the police to collect facts and act upon them. Valuable time had been lost and important clues destroyed. His summing up to the jury included a statement that said:

'the prisoner is entitled to the benefit of any doubt they might have in their minds, and referring to the fact that in English law there was no verdict of 'Not Proven', said, it did not follow that because a verdict of 'Not Guilty' was returned, it necessarily followed that the prisoner was innocent but merely that his guilt had not been established to their satisfaction beyond any reasonable doubt.'

It was clear, implied Wensley, that the judge, too, was sure of Healy's guilt, but the benefit of the doubt had been given. The detective reflected that the jury had been out for only twelve minutes. Surely that indicated they had made their mind up even before they had left the courtroom?

Not that it helped explain the verdict, but Wensley felt the need to add something about his reception in Hertfordshire, and it was something which would need addressing before any more of his colleagues suffered the same. Rural police forces at this time weren't sufficiently skilled to take on complex enquiries, and in particular murder cases where the guilt of the offender wasn't immediately apparent. Scotland Yard was therefore likely to be called in to assist chief constables with their enquiries in the future and Wensley wanted to bring to the attention of his senior officers some of the problems he had encountered. He outlined the conditions under which he had needed to operate and how he had been forced to work in a bitterly cold environment, at the scene of the crime, in an almost 'unendurable stench', and while he hadn't expected any, he didn't in fact receive any 'sympathetic assistance' from Superintendent Reed. He and his team had worked long hours on a daily basis and this proved to be a 'very severe test of physical endurance'.

Following on from this, Wensley offered his own opinion of the local police. He criticised the original poor control of the scene, and in particular how, had it been treated properly, important fingerprint evidence would have been obtained. When he inherited the investigation on 6 February, six witness statements had been taken and the case concluded. By the time the matter was brought to trial, he had taken ninety-three statements from sixty-seven witnesses both in England and Ireland.[109] He thought about Reed's words in his [Reed's] initial report: 'I have gone into every detail of the case very carefully and have no further particulars to report.' Bringing himself back to the task of writing his concluding report, he re-emphasised that before his arrival, everything had been 'obliterated and cleaned' and the publicity given to Reed's accident theory had prevented useful witnesses coming forward. Finally, he commended Sergeants Brewer and Cooper for their sustained efforts and in particular the evidence obtained from Ireland under very difficult circumstances. He also made particular mention of PC Waters, who 'took a keen interest in his work and rendered most useful assistance'.

Wensley submitted his musings, and his immediate senior officer, Superintendent Fred Thomas, endorsed the sentiment that Wensley being called in late rendered him 'badly handicapped from the start'. Had the matter been in his hands much sooner, he continued, he was quite sure that it would have resulted in a different verdict. He recommended Wensley for a commendation.

A few days later, at the request of Bedfordshire Police, Scotland Yard was called in to investigate the murder of Nellie Rault, who had been found stabbed to death on 12 May, some six weeks before. Wensley was given the case and he at once identified that this was yet again a matter in which Scotland Yard services should have been called for at a much earlier date. He made his way to Bedfordshire nervous about what he might find. Would the evidence all have been destroyed? What sort of welcome would he receive? His disquiet was reflected in the newspapers as they quickly heard that Wensley was on another case. *The Sketch* reported on 26 June that:

> 'if any man in Great Britain could unravel the tangled skein
> of mystery which surrounds the case, Mr Wensley is that man.
> Mr Wensley is one of the best detectives in the country and has
> a wonderful record of success. His failures during the many
> years he has been connected to the Metropolitan Police have
> been practically nil – his triumphs many. He holds the record
> in this country for the number of murderers he has arrested
> and until the Hitchin case had never lost a prisoner.'

Wensley stared at the article, but it was the last sentence that sent shivers down his spine.

> 'Whether he will succeed in Bedfordshire is an open question,
> for it is possible by this time that all the clues which might
> have led to arrest have been destroyed.'

His concerns were valid. Despite a thorough investigation, vital time had been lost and Nellie Rault's murderer was never brought to justice.

In the weeks that followed, there were a number of investigations carried out by Scotland Yard in county constabularies with unsuccessful outcomes, a fact highlighted by the *Daily Express* on 11 August 1919, when it reported that five people had now been murdered and that their killers remained at large. Public doubt was beginning to creep in on the ability of the police to catch the most serious offenders.

Wensley knew he had to take action and formally recommended that a specialist squad of selected officers be formed to assist not only with murder investigations in county forces but also to combat the growing trend of travelling criminals in the metropolis. In future, county chief constables would be required to call upon the services of the Metropolitan Police in cases of complexity, particularly murder investigations where the killer was not immediately apparent and to control criminality more effectively in London, the Flying Squad was formed.

In 1920, Wensley was awarded the MBE and became a leading figure, together with Francis Carlin, Arthur Neil and Albert Hawkins, the so-called 'Big Four', in some of the most notorious investigations throughout the 1920s.

Chapter 28

Thereafter

The first police officer on the scene of Elizabeth Ridgley's murder in January 1919, Alf Kirby, retired on 3 September 1919. He started as a constable; he finished as a constable.

Five months later, Wensley's dogged detective work and reshaping of the Metropolitan Police's CID reaped dividends when he was promoted to Chief Constable of Scotland Yard CID, the first officer to be so appointed having started as a constable. Regarded as the best detective the country had ever seen, the newspapers attributed his credibility to his grass-roots policing in the East End and the underworld of London being somewhat of an open book to him. Now awarded an OBE, he finally retired on 31 July 1929. He had served over forty years, worked tirelessly and had taken ninety-four sick days off work through injuries sustained on duty, each time being docked a shilling from his pay.

The Globe printed on 1 September 1928:

> 'Wensley's career as a detective has been a series of triumphs, characterised by a thoroughness that left little or no room for doubt in the minds of juries who have had to try his prisoners. He knew his East End better than any other police officer living and the promptitude with which he got to the bottom of the numerous murders entrusted to his investigation gave him a reputation of being gifted with second sight.'

Given the context of the Hitchin murder and Wensley's dealings with Healy, about which his wife herself had recorded that her husband was dealt with kindly, and Passingham's criticism of Wensley in the collection of his evidence, the remainder of the article had a certain resonance.

'Wensley is not the kind of man a murderer would wish to meet. One can never mistake the strong, dominating personality which is revealed at first glance. If he sets his heart on clearing up a crime it will be done, even if he has to work twenty-four hours in the day and keep his subordinates going for the same time. And although he possesses the reputation of being a martinet, he is one of the most popular men in the Metropolitan Police, because he never forgets that years ago he was a novice himself with everything to learn. His position at Scotland Yard today is unique and has no parallel in the history of the CID. For the past five or six years Wensley has been the man behind the scenes in solving practically every murder that has come within the range of the Metropolitan Police. Few of these cases have gone unpunished. It is not an unenviable task, this catching of murderers. There is always the probability that counsel for the defence will suggest, more or less openly, that the prisoner has been induced to make a "statement", which, in effect, resolves itself into a confession. Whatever may be the rights and wrongs of this subject, there will be no doubt in the public mind that the police are justified in doing everything within their powers to bring a murderer to justice. Police methods in England and Wales are scrupulously fair. We do not use the "Third Degree". Nor, fortunately, are we afflicted with the juge d'instruction who bellows at a man who does not at once confess his guilt. In this country, when a man is arrested and charged with a serious crime, he is warned that anything he says will be taken down in writing, and may be used in evidence. Scotland Yard's CID, always noted for efficiency, has become better than ever since Wensley became its controlling brain. Most of the old crooks considered it time to go out of business when he set to work. Today, for instance, the West-End of London is comparatively free from confidence tricksters. The old time "screwsmen" (burglars) have turned over a new leaf, while cheque forgers, once so flourishing, are behind prison walls. It would be unfair to other officers to attribute all this improvement to Mr Wensley even if one may think it a remarkable coincidence that this has taken place since he became "boss" of the CID. One of the secrets, perhaps, lies in his personal popularity with the rank and file. He has brought to Scotland Yard men who would never have had the chance of rising above the rank of detective inspector, had them promoted, and made them his principal assistants, eager and willing to carry out his wishes. Efficiency is certainly the watchword of the CID nowadays. At one time divisional officers never seriously troubled about a visit from the "The Governor". But Wensley is round and about his divisions regularly keeping a watchful eye on the staff and advising where necessary. Strangely enough, he is almost unknown by sight to the underworld, one of the reasons being that he does not walk about the streets and, at this stage of his career, never appears in court to give evidence. One might almost say he is the real power behind the police, although he allows his subordinates to reap the credit when a spectacular case is brought to a successful conclusion. But his power is none the less for that. He could walk about the West-End practically unrecognised, although the wary ones would sense danger in the square, determined chin and the unmistakable sternness which has come to him through long association of crime. It is remarkable that he never personally associates himself with a case. The trial of Louis Voison, the French butcher of Soho, was one of the last occasions when he gave evidence in court. The numerous sensational murder trials of the last six or seven years, notably the Vaquier case, the gruesome Eastbourne tragedy for which Patrick Mahon was hanged, the Crowborough chicken-farm case, the more recent episode of the woman Bonati whose dismembered body was found in the Charing Cross cloakroom were all the more remarkable for the fact that the man who directed operations remained practically unknown to the public.'

Dr Bernard Spilsbury carried on as Home Office pathologist, delighting juries and newspapers the length of the country and becoming widely regarded as brilliant and invincible. He appeared over two hundred times as a prosecution witness and received a knighthood in February 1923. But his haughty attitude attracted severe criticism to the extent that despite his obvious brilliance and integrity, his ability to get it right was often outweighed by the stubbornness he displayed when he got it wrong. As the years passed, newspapers started to question his conclusions in the face of conflicting evidence from other up-and-coming pathologists. By the 1930s, his reputation had started to crumble further when a judge stopped a trial as he considered Spilsbury's evidence purely speculative and not based on any scientific, medical reasoning. After another medical witness declared that 'when Spilsbury spoke of medical matters, he stopped listening,' he was hailed as fallible, even incompetent.

He took criticism badly and his unhealthy fifty cigarettes-a-day habit took its toll when, in 1940, while conducting a post mortem examination, he suffered a stroke. By this time, he was estranged from his wife, and a few months later, his son, Peter, also a doctor, died in a German bomb blast in London. However, despite depression setting in and him giving more of his time to freemasonry, he advised MI5 in 1943 in the renowned Operation Mincemeat disinformation plan to deceive the Axis powers into thinking that an allied attack would take place in Greece and Sardinia, paving the way clear for a successful invasion of Sicily. A corpse, approved by Spilsbury, was floated into the sea off the Spanish coast, his briefcase loaded with purposely false information in the hope the enemy would believe they had intercepted a genuine secret mission. The operation was successful and, arguably, it shortened the war by many months.

But later the same year he suffered another stroke. By 1944 he had significant financial worries and shortly after the Second World War one of his other sons died from tuberculosis. With his health deteriorating rapidly, his post mortem examinations were becoming increasingly careless, even on one occasion failing to notice a bullet fall from a victim's skull. More criticism was heaped upon him. Bereavement, overwork and an unhealthy lifestyle drained him, and on 17 December 1947 he committed suicide, gassing himself in his London laboratory. Despite his fame, his notoriety, his association with countless professionals, only twenty-two people mourned him at his funeral. He was seventy years old.

Sir Edward Marshall Hall, equally, continued to attract the attention of the newspapers, surrounding himself in controversy and accolade in equal measure. He quickly forgot his involvement in the Hitchin matter and the following year defended another ex-soldier charged with the murder of Bella Wright in Leicestershire, in what he would describe as his greatest case ever. Widely known as the 'Green Bicycle Murder', the defendant was faced with what appeared to be overwhelming evidence and his position looked hopeless when he chose to give evidence in his own defence. Marshall Hall, though, skilfully tore apart the prosecution case and, ironically, invited the jury to consider the matter to be one of a tragic accident. They agreed and acquitted the man who seemed destined for the hangman's noose.

The following year he defended a man charged with the particularly violent murder of a seventeen-year-old girl in Sussex. The 'Green Coat Murder' attracted the abhorrence of the public when the level of violence used became wider knowledge, and the jury, despite Marshall Hall's claim of mistaken identity, were quick to convict. For once, the 'Great Defender' didn't hide his own revulsion at the vileness of the attack and privately hoped the prisoner would hang. He was not disappointed.

His reputation, though, continued to build, if not for his involvement in the highest profile trials but for his theatrical outbursts. In 1921, in defending a man charged with several counts of administering drugs to procure an abortion, a nurse had made a fool of him in his cross-examination of her but he waited for his final address to the jury before getting his own back. He wanted to impress upon the jury that he considered this important witness to be a liar and, quoting from a play, aligned her to 'the fox, hyaena, crocodile and all beast of craft have been distilled to make one woman'. She was, he said, 'the origin of all the ills in the case.' It largely worked. The jury only convicted on one count.

As well as making routine appearances in court as a barrister, Marshall Hall also sat as a part-time judge at Guildford, but his career was nearing an end. Whether it was due to his deep-seated unhappiness or his health, which were the underlying causes, in February 1927, he died at the age of sixty-eight. No longer would the court actor entertain the public gallery.

In 1919, during that troubled period of post-war Britain, 35 million days were lost through strikes and industrial action. Trades union membership was nearing 8 million. Twelve people had a personal appearance with the hangman's noose; it so easily could have been thirteen. Of the 2,400 police officers who went out on strike in July 1919, none was ever allowed to work for the police again. Advertised vacancies in the early 1920s specifically stated that 'police strikers' need not apply. Despite numerous pleas to different Home Secretaries, their pensions were never reinstated, and many families of the once low-paid police officers embarked upon an even harder and hungrier life and passed into history.

John Healy made it plain that he felt he wasn't welcome in the Hertfordshire town and left the area immediately, eventually returning to Ireland. The country was in turmoil. Catholic sentiment in the south hardened towards British control, and despite an agreement to retain six counties in the north of the country under British rule, animosity grew between the different supporters. Part of the government's response to the situation was the introduction of the Black and Tans, a police auxiliary group characterised by violence and which in turn garnered anti-police sentiment, something that was very noticeable in Listowel with the local police commander instructing his officers to shoot on sight any suspicious persons and with no questions being asked. Hunger strikers, he said, had 'already been dealt with in a manner their friends would never hear about. Sinn Fein had had all the sport up to present, but the police were going to have the sport now.'

A violent civil war had broken out, resulting in over a thousand people being killed before Northern Ireland became formalised in 1922. Five years later, on 20 May, and eight years after Elizabeth Ridgley was murdered, while employed as a farmer, John Healy died of double pneumonia after a ten-day illness in his home town of Listowel.[110] He was forty years old. He was buried in St Michael's graveyard, in an unmarked grave mourned by Annie and his tong-wielding brother, Thomas. Despite all that was said about their fractious relationship, his wife had remained at his side, but at a relatively young age, the Listowel's farmer's brush with the world war and the small town of Hitchin ended. He too passed into history.

It is not known what retired Superintendent George Reed thought about the events of 1919 after his retirement. Despite the evidence that came to light after his initial investigation, following the acquittal of Healy, he may well have concluded, as he had originally thought, that Elizabeth Ridgley died as a result of a tragic accident. We may never know.

Chapter 29

Author's Commentary

It could be argued that to re-examine a murder investigation a hundred years after its commission is unhelpful. Least of all it would be quite wrong to look at it from a present-day perspective. That is the beautiful thing about history; trying to show exactly what happened using original material and putting it in a contemporary social setting so that the reader can better understand and make sense of it all. I hope that the narrative has not only thrown light on policing in the early part of the century but portrayed it as a piece of history and not as retrospective critique.

But as I researched this rather extraordinary affair and repeatedly read the case papers, it was obvious that there were gaps in the information, making it difficult even for me, someone who has investigated murders, to try and piece it all together. I didn't want the book to end leaving the reader with a sense of unfulfillment – too many unanswered questions – and perhaps my biggest concern, granting a licence to the readers of this book to start using their imagination and invent theories that are better left to the crime novelist. Thus, in this final chapter I analyse these gaps and attempt to provide a greater understanding of early twentieth century police investigations and address those lurking questions.

Policing in 1919

The aftermath of the First World War without doubt left a skills shortage in a workplace dominated by men. Three quarters of a million men had lost their lives, and those who survived returned to find that women had filled their jobs and were knocking on the door of universal suffrage; Britain had changed. It would be fair to say that the police service suffered in a similar vein, though the numbers killed were far less. Of the eighty-five Hertfordshire police officers who joined the military during the 1914–18 war, nine were killed and many others seriously wounded. Large city forces were able to absorb the impact far more easily than the counties, but nonetheless it is difficult to conclude that after the war the police service was so stripped of experienced officers that it was a wholesale practical problem. Indeed, it was probably more of a problem for metropolitan and borough forces like the Metropolitan Police and the Borough of Liverpool Police after many had been sacked after the police strikes of 1918 and 1919, which created a skills shortage for many years to come. Certainly, this is an argument put forward by some authors for the reason behind the failed investigation in Liverpool of the murder of Julia Wallace in 1931.

All the police officers who first attended 125, Nightingale Road on Monday, 27 January 1919, were experienced; but experienced in what? In many ways, the war had forced the Home Office to take its eyes off the police service, and the disparate approaches adopted by the many small forces did nothing to develop a homogenised and systemic approach to good practice. Indeed, policing was still seen as a local function, with foot patrol being the basis of all good police work. In Hertfordshire, Chief Constable Law was still emphasising the importance of drill, a function that officers should embrace with some pride; clearly a legacy of the war and symptomatic of the militaristic philosophy still engrained in policing. When war had broken out, the police assumed a wide range of new duties under emergency legislation, suddenly required to arrest enemy aliens, guard vulnerable points, apprehend deserters, check up on wives who were claiming a separation allowance, often fraudulently, and enforce lighting restrictions. None of these, though, had any lasting effects after hostilities ended, and the more mundane returned, with the requirement to enforce drunkenness, assaults and dishonesty.

Hertfordshire, though, had dealt with few murders, about a dozen over as many years, but it is worthy of note that it had dealt with a significant case which would have resonated with the Ridgley investigation. In 1899, Mercy Nicholls had been murdered in the street and onlookers simply did nothing, allowing her killer to finish his task. The *Hertfordshire Mercury* wrote an article, asking how 'in the midst of a thoroughfare crowded with inhabitants a woman could be brutally done to death without one living human being raising his hand to help her … Is the age of manliness and chivalry dead in Hertford?' Two constables were dismissed for negligence and the superintendent came in for criticism for failing to attend. At the time it galvanised the then chief constable into action by creating, according to the local newspaper, 'one of the most efficient forces in the country.'

Since the war though, police forces had become used to more centralised control, which led to the formation of chief constable conferences in the Home Office. These meetings acted as a means of exchanging ideas and experiences, which was without doubt the catalyst for Scotland Yard sending memos to rural chief constables encouraging them to seek support where necessary, murder investigations in particular. But in the immediate aftermath of the war, 1919 in particular, it would be fair to say that police forces were in a sickly state.

The initial investigation

Despite, or perhaps because of a lurking Victorian attitude towards policing, what is incredible is that when Constable Kirby first found the body of Elizabeth Ridgley, he very soon came to a conclusion that she had been murdered. Indeed, one of the neighbours accompanying him into the house, Edwin Sutton, a taxi driver, even commented that he thought 'she's been done in'. That message remained clear until it reached Inspector Bowyer, since the first piece of information he received was that a woman had been 'murdered'. What is not clear and simply cannot be ascertained is the dialogue that subsequently took place between that 'conspiracy of officers', Reed, Warren and Bowyer over the next forty-eight hours. Kirby had already concluded murder, though his thoughts were somewhat suppressed by his inspector. Sergeant Boarder appears to be on the brink of a conspiracy of silence by describing Ridgley's clothes as 'more or less bloodstained' and the two inspectors then take over. The extent to which Kirby's previous attendance at the house in the summer of 1918 and what he had said about it to his supervisors thereby influencing events from there on in, will always be a moot point. Did Kirby unwittingly sow the seed that this was a woman, a drunk woman (of which there is no evidence at all), who had probably taken a fall, and his bosses simply accepted that and started to misinterpret the scene? Worse still, once they had formulated that opinion, did they, in turn, ignoring what the medical examination had revealed, brief Reed along the same lines? In other words, before the superintendent had even stepped over the threshold he knew he was going into a house where a drunken woman had, once again, fallen down, but this time killed herself.

Before we explore further the reasoning of Superintendent Reed, it is interesting that on the police file in the National Archives is a short, typed report, which by its nature and content can be dated (although it is undated) to prior to Wensley's arrival on 6 February. I would suggest that it was authored by one of the inspectors and reads:

> 'DEATH OF MRS RIDGLEY AT HITCHIN. Mrs Roach appears to have made, according to her statement, what may be described as a faint-hearted attempt to call attention to certain groans which she heard on Saturday between 11 and 12pm – she did this presumably as being indicative of something being wrong. She explains that she thought the groans might have proceeded from the house opposite from some soldier billeted there who might have had tooth-ache.
>
> 'On Sunday Mrs Roach's son told her that Mrs Ridgley's back door was open, she apparently did not think it necessary to inform anybody because she explains the back door was nearly always open, nevertheless, considering all the circumstances it seems to be a matter of enquiry why Mrs Roach took no steps on Sunday to resume her enquiries or to inform her neighbours or the police.'

Roach's ambivalence was first discovered by PC Kirby, when he took a statement from her at 11.30am on the morning that Ridgley was discovered. I would suggest that he expressed incredulity at her complacency or bitterness towards the deceased and brought it to his inspectors' attention. But it appears that this extraordinary behaviour was seen as just that; extraordinary behaviour. Had she intervened earlier, she may, as it appears to have been interpreted, have gone into the shop and discovered Mrs Ridgley's accidental fall. It certainly didn't indicate murder.

So, let's give Reed the benefit of the doubt and for now at least give him the partial excuse that he had been misinformed. He looked around the premises, saw a seemingly disorganised household, noted the beer on the table, blood all over the place and no evidence of any money having been stolen. At this time, having not yet seen the body, he could see that the accidental death theory appeared to be looking reasonable. If that had been the extent of it, it can be seen how a mistake could have been made. But there was this rather sticky issue of a dead dog and a four-pound weight resting on the floor in the passageway of the house. The two inspectors had formed the opinion that the hairs on the weight were not human, but how could they have drawn such a concrete conclusion – they weren't medical men. Bowyer would later add that Ridgley's clothes were not 'disarranged or torn.' The dynamics inside that household were interesting. Was it the two inspectors forming an opinion and trying to impress upon their superintendent exactly how death had occurred or was it Reed's presence and unrecorded mutterings which effectively cajoled the two officers into downplaying their interpretation. In any event it matters not. Reed was the senior officer, he had attended the scene and it was for him, and him alone, to make a judgement. But let's be fair to him. From the moment he arrived it looks as though he was being misled about this poor, drunken old woman who had fallen over and somehow killed her dog in the process.

Quite where the next part of the theory originates is impossible to tell, but Reed must assume responsibility for it. Somehow, he wrote in his report, Ridgley had probably killed her dog with either the weight or the broom. The blood on the broom handle proved that and the absence of human hairs on the weight supported it. The shopkeeper had regained consciousness and wandered around the shop dropping blood all over the place. Remember, the dog was already dead or dying at this time. But there was no blood or dog motion on the soles of the shoes of the dead woman despite there being three piles of it in close proximity to where her body was found. If it wasn't apparent at the scene, although it appears it was, surely the clenched fists of the victim, which would have been seen at the mortuary, were indicative of someone in great fear at the time of her death and not someone who was drunk and smashing her dog over the head with a broom or four-pound weight. Equally, if the victim had been using a handkerchief to try and stem the flow of blood, how would it end up being 'tied loosely around the neck?' And finally, if she had fallen or stumbled, why were the victim's feet perpendicular to the floor, her heels pointing upwards and toes downwards? Did that not look odd?

But, at the very least, he surely must have been convinced that this was *probably* murder, given the three main factors; a dead woman with her head smashed in, a dead dog with its head smashed in and a four-pound lump of iron resting between the two bodies. Blood all over the place, including on the bolt of the front door, would have been an extra clue, but by now, murder should have been suspected. Far easier to scream murder and then disprove it than the other way round. It should have been that a taxi driver, a constable or a police superintendent with thirty-two years' service would have realised that these factors point away from the accidental death theory. Regrettably, it was only the superintendent who missed or ignored the point.

This lack of clarity in thinking and logic sits alongside the indifference displayed by Reed and his two inspectors as they walked around the property indiscriminately picking up items – not least the bloodstained cigar box and cardboard receptacle – in their search for clues. But did they know what they were looking for? It is not a quantum leap to suggest that their priority should have been to protect the scene, not disturb it, and this was clearly in Kirby's mind, who took steps to ensure that little was moved. This was not the first murder in Hertfordshire and Reed would have been well aware, like his constable, that preservation of the scene was paramount. In his statement, Inspector Warren makes mention of a chamber pot underneath the dining room table which had a great deal of blood collected in it, but Wensley is highly doubtful of the integrity of this statement due to the lack of other blood in the area and felt sure that it had been moved by someone; Grellett, Boarder, Sutton, Wheeler or Bowyer. Wensley's suspicion about the moving of items in the house is reinforced when he noticed that Reed specifically mentioned a bloodstained broom in the living room. Kirby made no mention of this and Mary Chandler had clearly indicated to him that it was normally kept in the scullery area.[111] Warren's attitude and approach to the whole investigation can perhaps be seen in his comment in his statement when he said that 'he understood that the deceased was suffering from wounds on the face and head.' Understood? Was he closely involved in this investigation or not? Today, it is almost comedic, when reading Bowyer's statement describing how Reed examined the scene by candlelight, that 'it threw no light on the matter.'

The next crucial factor in Reed starting to go down the wrong road is when the doctor told him that *some* of the injuries *could* have been caused by a fall, albeit he seemingly followed this up, according to Wensley, with an unequivocal statement saying that Ridgley had been murdered. So, why did the doctor introduce the doubt? He was being clear with Reed, that of course it was likely that some of the more superficial injuries were consistent with falling onto the packaged utensils, but the cause of death was the significant fracture to the skull. This particular aspect of the evidence is fascinating, since nowhere in Grellett's statements does he actually say that Ridgley had a fractured skull or was indeed murdered. It is not even clear when he made his first statement as it is not dated. This throws up an interesting question. When exactly did he draw this conclusion about murder? The only reference to him offering this opinion is in the report of Wensley, dated 15 February, when he apparently said, 'he had not the slightest doubt that it was a case of murder'.[112] An equally compelling piece of evidence is that Reed concedes in his report that the injuries, according to Grellett, could 'be the result of being struck a severe blow by some person'. There must have been an unrecorded conversation between the doctor and the superintendent because Reed says in his report that Ridgley has died as a result of a fractured skull, yet this doesn't feature in Grellett's written statement. Since the medical aspects of the case were taken over later by Spilsbury, this unsatisfactory fudge is not something that was subjected to court scrutiny.

Now, none of this excuses Reed's seemingly 'fixed-theory analysis' and his blatant disregard of the entirety of the evidence, but it becomes clearer that having been told that Ridgley was a drunken old woman susceptible to the occasional fall, he is told by the doctor, as far as all the statements are concerned, that some of the injuries may have been caused by a fall; indeed, the fracture may have been caused by a fall. His theory gains momentum when Goldsmith, the veterinary surgeon, expresses the view that he does *not* think the injuries to the dog were caused by the four-pound weight, although it was definitely the blows to the back of the head which killed it. However, it is not until Wensley arrives in Hitchin that a statement is eventually taken from the vet, on 13 February, and he confirms his earlier conclusion.

When the exhumation and subsequent post mortem of Ridgley confirms the murder theory, and that the weight is the likely weapon, it appears that Goldsmith is not re-interviewed nor does he appear to have been challenged in court over his opinion that the four-pound weight wasn't the cause of death, particularly after Spilsbury examined the animal and found the fracture to the skull. This is remarkable for two reasons. Firstly, this was a perfect opportunity for Healy's defence team to show that while the prosecution case was that the weight was the cause of death to both Mrs Ridgley and her dog, here was a medical expert saying that the weight didn't kill her pet. Therefore, considerable doubt transfers to the cause of death of the shopkeeper. It would have been the perfect defence on a plate; Spilsbury saying that more than likely the weight killed both and Grellett contradicting that. Doubt would have been sown in the minds of the jury. The second point, however, is even more striking. Given that Grellett stated to Reed that the four-pound weight didn't cause the injuries to the dog, how can the vet's evidence in all the subsequent court proceedings be explained? He didn't give evidence at the opening of the inquest, although he was reported in the newspapers to have said to Reed that the injuries to the dog were as a result of 'a lucky shot'. At the final inquest hearing, he agreed that the dog had been 'struck silly'. At the remand hearing on 4 March, however, after Spilsbury's examination of the dog, Grellett told the court that the dog had received 'two or three blows causing the head to fracture'. He is not asked, 'With what?' Was it because the prosecutor knew that Goldsmith would stick with his story, thereby undermining the prosecution case, or would it have caused considerable embarrassment to acknowledge he may have been wrong. Of course, it lends itself to another theory, that it was Reed who convinced the vet that the weight wasn't the fatal instrument, but there is no evidence at all of such a corrupt act. In Wensley's report to the Director of Public Prosecutions, he alludes to the fact that Reed's questioning of Dr Grellett about the injuries to Mrs Ridgley makes it quite clear that the superintendent thought this an accidental death. It is not difficult therefore to extend this thinking to the conservation between Reed and Goldsmith. Perhaps the one fact that strikes at the heart of this issue is that having been told by Reed he may dispose of the carcase of the dog, he didn't. Either he simply hadn't got round to it before he received a further call from the police or he knew he was wrong. It was his way of clawing back poor judgement.

The final cut-off point to rescue this deplorable investigation was that after the complacent approach to walking around the house, picking up items indiscriminately and ultimately obliterating potential fingerprints, Ridgley's family is given carte blanche to clean up. At that juncture, the investigation was doomed.

One matter which stands out and is of interest is the amount of newspaper articles citing murder. On the day after Ridgley's body was found, and therefore before Reed had carried out his investigation, national newspapers were leading with unequivocal headlines; HITCHIN WOMAN'S DEATH – SUSPICION OF MURDER printed *The Times*, and the *Daily Sketch* emblazoned, MYSTERY OF MURDERED WOMAN, LONELY SHOPKEEPER'S TRAGIC FATE AT HITCHIN. FACE BADLY MUTILATED, DOG FOUND POISONED BESIDE MISTRESS'S BODY. Amazingly, three days later, and after the opening of the inquest and now four days into Reed's investigation, the *Daily Sketch* again pursued the murder theory; HITCHIN MURDER MYSTERY. Reporting on the post mortem, its next line read, NOW INDISPUTABLE THAT A HEAVY BLOW TO THE TOP OF THE HEAD WAS THE CAUSE OF DEATH. On 1 February, one of the local papers, the *Hertfordshire Mercury*, led with, MURDER FEARED AT HITCHIN – SHOPKEEPER'S TRAGIC DEATH.

There are two points here which stand out prominently. Firstly, how did Reed reconcile his developing thoughts when at the same time the newspapers were reporting murder? He would have had little or no control over national newspapers but quite a lot of influence over what appeared in local articles. Thus, the second point; who was providing them with information? Reed had taken control of the investigation by nightfall on 27 January, but despite this, the journalists were aware of the extent of the injuries, the probable cause of death and by what means, and the fact that the dog had most likely been poisoned – which it hadn't. This last issue was Kirby's initial theory based on the froth next to the dog's mouth, and he had specifically asked that this avenue be explored by the veterinary surgeon, Goldsmith. So was it Kirby who was pushing the murder agenda, or perhaps Boarder, or any number of loose-lipped constables in Hitchin Division? By the time the *Hertfordshire Mercury* reported on 1 February, they had got the details from the inquest, a public forum. So at some time between 1 and 2 February, when he penned his report, Reed had drawn his conclusion.

There was a four-day window between Reed concluding his report and Wensley arriving in Hertfordshire, ample time for the superintendent to put the record straight and declare it an accident. So, did he? Well, he possibly tried. On 8 February, the *Bedfordshire Express* changed its language to THE HITCHIN MYSTERY. The word murder had disappeared. It even printed that there was still no explanation of the death of Mrs Ridgley and 'none is expected even after the adjourned inquest date of 19 February'. Yet this line of journalism wasn't taken up by any other newspaper, local or national. It would have been an interesting dilemma facing the editors; initially a suspected murder, then an accident and now Scotland Yard called in. What did all this mean?

Before I move on to my analysis of the second investigation, it is important to clear up one point. When Superintendent Reed composed his report to the Chief Constable, he stated that the sum of money found in the living room amounted to £12.5s.1½d, whereas Constable Kirby, at that time, had only found £9.11s. Similarly, when Reed handed the money over to the family, he quoted a larger figure than that documented by Kirby. For the sake of clarity, I do not read anything sinister into that and it is more than likely that by the time Reed wrote his report, more money had been found on the premises; the majority of it comprised threepenny pieces. There is though, no record of this (or at least none now exists) but it may be symptomatic of the indifference displayed from the outset of the investigation.

The second investigation

In the nine days between arriving in Hitchin and the arrest of Healy, Wensley made good progress. He must have quietly rejoiced, knowing that the till boxes and weight hadn't been thrown away by Mrs Chandler and this was perhaps the single factor which could rescue the situation. Wrong as it turned out, but he must have reconstructed the scene with a sense of expectation and optimism. Spilsbury had clearly used the precipitin test to determine that the blood found on Healy's clothes was human and not animal. Had there been animal blood on his clothes it would have been implied that this belonged to the dead dog, so carrying out the test was vital. However, despite a process that had been developed in 1901 by Dr Karl Landsteiner, which enabled human blood to be categorised into different groups, (A, B, AB and O) and which was used to facilitate the successful transfusion of blood on First World War battlefields, this test was seemingly not employed. In the 1927 Charing Cross murder, where the dismembered body of Minnie Bonati was found in a trunk, where a bloodstained matchstick was found in the suspect's house and where the use of blood grouping would have been exceptionally helpful, there was no mention of the use of this technique. In fact, the use of blood grouping in a criminal trial doesn't appear to have been used until as late as 1932, in the case of *R v Freedman,* despite the science being available. If Ridgley and Healy had different blood groups and both had been found at the scene, the case would have been all but proven.

However, Wensley identified that Mrs Ridgley met her death in a violent manner unwittingly overheard by the neighbour and established that robbery was the motive. Paradoxically, this romantic notion of motive is not a necessary factor in proving murder, nor indeed any crime. But it helps. The one thing, though, that the detective didn't establish for nine days was the identity of a suspect. It was more by luck than judgement that further evidence wasn't lost (if you believe that John Healy was the murderer), largely brought about by the residents of Hitchin thinking that Mrs Ridgley had met her death by accident. When Wensley and his team went through the front door of 16, Radcliffe Road, they were greeted by a display of circumstantial evidence; bloodstained clothing and bedding, a pipe, some tell-tale cuts to the prisoner's hand and a wife who spoke of her missing husband on the night of the murder and who had some khaki handkerchiefs. Had Wensley been provided with more staff or Reed done his job properly, with Healy only living two hundred yards away, it is more than likely that the Smith family, with their knowledge of events, would have been found and spoken up earlier. Had they done so, one of two things would have happened. Either Healy would have been arrested sooner than 15 February or panic would have set in and anything that could have connected him to the murder would have been destroyed. We will never know, of course, but it looks likely that Wensley did everything he reasonably could.

For me, a particularly interesting aspect of the case, is how Wensley stumbled across Healy in the first place. From a document written after the trial, I could ascertain that Wensley had received a letter pointing him in the direction of the Irishman. The letter, however, no longer exists and its exact content therefore is not known. The obvious question is: who wrote the letter? There are a number of options but my feeling is that, even if it was anonymous, it was written by Mavis Smith. On the face of it, her mother, Annie, could not write and the detailed information which was contained in the letter must have come from the Smith household. Perhaps, an unimportant point, but one that needs highlighting.

One thing intrigues me, though, and I cannot come up with a logical explanation. When Wensley decided to go to the newspapers to announce that he was now dealing with a murder investigation, he itemised a number of points about which he sought information. Asking for any sightings about a suspicious bloodstained man using bloodstained Treasury notes is understandable, but why was he quite so specific about 'any man who wanted his forearm or hand – probably the left – dressed'? Why was he so sure about the murderer's left hand being cut and not, as in fact it transpired with Healy, the right hand? It could be that the detective and the pathologist reconstructed events at the house trying to work out in detail how a man could have possibly inflicted fatal blows to two victims and came to a conclusion about where he must have been standing during the attack. Certainly, the location of blood spattering would have indicated where the shopkeeper was when she was attacked and even possibly the dog itself. But there are so many variables around this that no firm conclusion can be drawn. Was he basing it on the likelihood that the attacker was probably right-handed, necessitating the use of his left hand to protect himself from attack by the animal? Despite those in charge at Scotland Yard questioning this aspect – even annotating the file with the question, 'Why left hand?' – it is a point which appears not to have been probed or even exploited by Healy's defence barrister during the course of the trial.

The question of motive lingers on most crime enthusiasts' lips. As I said earlier, this is not a prerequisite to proving the commission of a crime but it of course helps the casual observer and even a juror to form an opinion. In Healy's case, the motive was money. He and his wife had little means, but in particular he was, in his own words 'broke' before the murder and, said the prosecution, had plenty afterwards. This was a double-edged sword, since Healy argued, truthfully, that he received an army gratuity the week after the murder and before he settled his outstanding debts. So, to use his sudden possession of money was not the strongest of propositions and we are not in a position to say whether paying his rent and buying new clothes was as a result of stealing it from Nightingale Road or whether it was as a result of a state pay-out. However, if the Smiths are to be believed, he was drunk on the two evenings following the murder and so must have come into money somehow. But this is all an aside to something which emerged as the witnesses told their stories. It is not beyond the realms of possibility that Healy grew to dislike Ridgley. He was short of money. She had, by comparison, a great deal. He was not a benevolent person by any standards, and his comment about how he felt no sympathy towards how she had met her death was either because he had become desensitised by the atrocities of war or he was, in any event, a violent individual who thought nothing about thumping his way through life. He was a regular drunk, had been charged but acquitted of a violent robbery nine years earlier in Ireland, was cruel to animals and routinely engaged in violence in the Healy household in that isolated corner of a cow field.

We know that the Healys owed money to the grocer and she went about the town in search of the family trying to find their new address. They owed her 4s.7d, a small proportion of the Healy weekly wage, and she was told by two people that they had moved to Radcliffe Road. She had also been told by Catherine Lawrence to not be afraid of Healy and the next time he came into the shop she should challenge him. She even left a demand note at the address and which Annie Healy paid in part on the day of the murder. Healy's attitude towards his wife was cruel and violent and his temper flared most prominently when money was the subject of conversation. Knowing about the demand note from Ridgley may have been the last straw and one which heightened his resolve. With a sense of being hunted and embarrassed by Ridgley, and possibly knowing his wife was visiting the shop that night to pay off part of the debt, could it be that he set his heart on stealing from the shop but which, through bad luck, ended in murder? Once he had tried to rifle the till, had been unsuccessful and Ridgley chanced upon his thieving activities, he metaphorically killed two birds with one stone. Ridgely and her pet dog were finished off and he was £10 better off. A successful night out.

This was a period in history when the police were regarded as the good chasing the bad and they should employ whatever means were possible to ensure someone was convicted and hanged. This point is amply illustrated in the *Globe* newspaper article about Wensley's retirement, when it said, 'the police are justified in doing everything within their powers to bring a murderer to justice'. Wensley himself would later state in 1931:

> 'If the business of the detective is to detect criminals, he must be allowed reasonable attitude in performing his duty, although I am far from advocating that he should be permitted to go outside the limits of the law, fair play or common sense. He should be allowed to feel supported and encouraged in his efforts to protect the community.'[113]

So, let us now examine two of the key issues which stand out in this matter; the interview of John Healy and the evidence of William Augustus Craswell.

There is no need to fully re-rehearse the argument put forward at the remand hearings by Healy's solicitor George Passingham. In summary, he argued that the statement obtained from Healy was unlawful. He was neither arrested nor cautioned and yet a statement was obtained from him which provided a major plank of the subsequent investigation. Only *after* that was he arrested and advised that he need not say anything. The law at this time was unclear, and indeed remained so for many years. The Judges' Rules, which governed the arrest, cautioning and interview of suspects, was 'advisory' rather than mandatory. In other words, providing a police officer could justify it, the rules need not be complied with. This led to a situation where people were asked to accompany police officers to the police station. There they were asked questions and this led to them making a written statement. Not in all cases, but in many, the person was then charged with murder and only then was he told that he need not say anything unless he wished to do so and that whatever he said may be used in evidence. Too late. The 'confession' is damning and obtained without any measure of protection. The Judges' Rules were introduced for this very reason, to protect people from incriminating themselves in accusations of committing a crime. I think it is fair to say that Wensley was following accepted police procedure, but Passingham was, quite correctly, applying the letter of the law.

The issue hinges on, as indeed Wensley argued in court, that at the time of questioning there was no evidence of him having committed a crime and therefore no need to administer a caution. Indeed, he wasn't even told why he was required to go the police station;[114] the law didn't require it even if arrested. But, as Passingham pointed out, if there was no evidence of the person having committed a crime – in other words, there was no suspicion – why was Healy taken to the police station, placed in a police cell and his house searched? In truth, he *was* suspected, he *was* interviewed and more by luck said nothing which put his neck in the noose. Let us ask the ultimate question; if he had refused to go to the police station, would he have been arrested? I suggest he would. Moreover, once at the police station and before he had made his statement, if he had chosen to leave, would he have been allowed to? I suggest he would not. Does this loose interpretation of the guidelines fall into Wensley's categorisation of the detective being 'allowed reasonable attitude in performing his duty?' Is this what was meant by the *Globe* newspaper when it proclaimed, 'the police are justified in doing everything within their powers to bring a murderer to justice?' The key phrase here, of course, is 'within their powers'.

This analysis of Healy's arrest and interview is not a twenty-first century author looking back into history. The rules in 1919 were based upon the very case that Wensley himself was involved in, *R v Voison* (1917), and which was ultimately decided upon in the Court of Appeal. There was perhaps no other police officer in Britain more acutely aware of the requirements of arresting, cautioning and interviewing a prisoner than Detective Chief Inspector Wensley, and in his memoirs, he is clearly sensitive to this particular aspect of police procedure. In recalling the arrest of Frederick Bywaters in 1922, he almost boasts about administering a caution before the prisoner was interviewed, and in the same year, in detailing the arrest of Herbert Armstrong, he cites that the suspect was invited to make a statement 'after the usual warning.' Had Wensley followed this procedure in his dealings with Healy, Passingham would not have been able to object. Perhaps, three years later, Wensley had learned his lesson.

Before leaving this aspect of the investigation, it is worth quoting Wensley's own views on this important legal point, which he obviously felt deeply enough to spend some time on in his book:

'It is the truth that no police officer can compel anyone to answer his questions. That point has, I think, been injudiciously advertised. But to say he shall ask no questions when suspicion concentrates on a particular individual is not only to violate common sense but would frequently result in great moral injustice to the person concerned. I have known it happen hundreds of times that the first study of a case would appear to implicate some man who, when seen and questioned, has been able to establish his innocence. It frequently occurs that, as an inquiry develops, three or four people are under suspicion in turn. They have to be questioned by someone – and it appears to me that it is in the interests of those innocently concerned that it should be done by a discreet police officer rather than with the formality and, maybe, with all the publicity of a court. The futility of this has been seen in some cases where coroners have subjected certain witnesses to severe examination on points that appeared suspicious. Really it is for the police to find the criminal.

'It is a confusion of thought that regards any department of administration of the criminal law as engaged in a sort of game in which every guilty person shall be shielded in every possible way from betraying himself. The true principle is that no-one should be forced to incriminate himself – quite a different thing.'

Recognising Wensley's undoubted integrity of purpose in the way he went about his investigations, in the Healy case it is clear he was balancing on the fence; on the one hand wanting to get an account from someone who he clearly regarded as guilty, on the other, knowing that such an account must be obtained within the law.

Now let us consider the evidence of William Augustus Craswell. His story is really quite remarkable. Arguably, he was the most important witness in the entire case. By implication, he saw the murderer, provided the lead about him buying the tobacco and matches, described him (poorly, defence counsel argued), later recognised his photo in the *Daily Sketch*, and told someone who he genuinely thought was a police officer, albeit a journalist of questionable integrity as it turned out, what he now knew. His evidence at the trial gave everyone a shock when he unexpectedly blasted out, 'I tried to make a doubt about seeing him in case I should be called to try and pick him.' Notwithstanding that this did not become clear until during the trial, as soon as Craswell had come forward to say he had seen a man in the shop at the relevant time, he should have been regarded as a witness who could identify a man in a shop just before a murder. He came forward on 7 February and Healy was arrested on 15 February. That should have been the time that an identification parade should have been held.

He did not disclose his new evidence about recognising Healy from a photograph in a newspaper until 3 March, which may have influenced Wensley's view about the worth of holding a parade. In other words, there was a risk that Craswell would only identify the man in the newspaper photo rather than the man he had seen in the shop, the very same reason why there was no need for either Mavis Smith or Jens Christiansen, who saw Healy outside the shop, to attend, as they would simply have picked out John Healy, the man they lived with. But does that have any bearing on Craswell's ability to attend an identification parade between 15 February and 3 March?

Before I explore this any further, the history of the identification of suspects needs to be understood. The subject of identification, like police cautions, was prominent in criminal justice circles in 1919. The root of doubt about the value of identification evidence and the vagaries of human beings with their varied ability to remember faces was established during Wensley's early career. In the 1890s, in London, where the fledgling detective was learning his trade, Adolph Beck was being routinely arrested for crimes he didn't commit. Not only arrested, but convicted and imprisoned. Only once he was suspected of another crime at a time when he was already in prison was it realised that a mistake had been made. Repeatedly, he had been mistakenly identified by different witnesses, and at a time when there was no method of appealing against a conviction. This sequence of miscarriages of justice led to the creation of the Court of Appeal in 1907, and in future, judges were required to warn juries about the unreliability of identification evidence. Identification parades had been used for decades – indeed, Beck took part in them himself – and despite recognising the weaknesses of the process it remained the preferred method of identifying a suspect rather than a dock identification at the time of trial; at least there were a number of other similar-looking people alongside the suspect.

Knowing this, what would Wensley's thinking have been in the knowledge that Craswell had seen the tobacco and matches man? Was this man a suspect? Possibly not, but he needed to be identified. But it is right to say that we don't know what dialogue took place between police officers and witnesses. We only know that Craswell claimed that he wished to sow doubt into people's minds about his ability to recognise the man. If he had indeed told Sergeant Brewer that he wouldn't be able to recognise the man, then it would be reasonable to not ask him to attend an identification parade. But if it was a genuinely held belief that Craswell would not be capable of making an identification, why was he then asked at the remand hearing on 4 March, the day after he made his surprise disclosure to the police, whether the prisoner in the dock was the man? And of course, he positively identified him, much to the exasperation of the defendant on trial. I venture to suggest that the prosecutor, Sims, was aware that Craswell had indicated that he would now recognise Healy, hence the leading questions put to him:

'Have you seen him since?'
'Not until today.'
'Is he in court?'
'He is the prisoner.'

If my assumption is correct, surely it would have been better to have carried out an identification parade before his being asked this question in court; it would have been in the interests of justice to delay the witness giving his evidence and would have provided the jury at the later trial with identification evidence that had a deal more integrity. If my assumption is wrong, then it was a very risky question to put to a witness. If Craswell had said that he did not recognise the prisoner as the man in the shop, the prosecution case starts to crumble. It may well be, of course, and we will never know, that it was Craswell's prevarication which provided the doubt in the jury's mind.

Again, Wensley applied his mind to this matter in his memoirs:

'Another line of thought that, to me, seems muddled is in regard to methods of identification. I do not believe that anything can prevent an honestly mistaken identification. There are people who have unquestionably got doubles in appearance, action and speech. They might be wrongly recognised in any circumstances, under any precautions. In practical detective work what happens is this: A man who has been responsible for a crime has been seen by one or more people who say that they would know him again, and can give some sort of description. It is very difficult for the ordinary person to give a description of someone who he may have only seen once, and one has to consider how far a particular witness has been likely to observe and remember and is capable of conveying an impression. Age, for instance, is very deceptive. Women are apt to be hazy about heights. Yet, after giving a totally misleading description, people may, and not infrequently do, recognise a suspect directly they are brought face to face.'

'Usually, however, there is some characteristic that has consciously or unconsciously impressed a witness. It may be that he stutters, has a scar, or a wooden leg, or is cross-eyed. It may be something trifling, such as the way in which he walks, a manner of holding the head or swinging the arms or even something that may be called atmosphere. Some wide general impression may be quite as effective in recalling a person as a detailed description.

'When an identification of a suspect is made, it is because he is different in some characteristic from other people. He is remembered, perhaps, because that characteristic is a striking one, and here is one of the points about identification parades that are frequently criticised by ill-informed people. Ten or a dozen people of apparently the same age, build and station in life, are invited to take part, and the suspect stands where he will among them. It has been seriously argued that there should be a special resemblance in every detail among those with whom he stands. This would really make every attempt at identification a perfect farce. One very careful provincial officer who carried out an identification was ironically asked by Mr Justice Swift whether the people concerned were allowed to wear false beards and to black their faces ...

'The fact is that in London all identification parades are conducted with extreme fairness – and usually the person who least of all wants a man wrongly identified is the person in charge of the case, to whom a mistake may mean endless work and trouble. It should also be remembered that in every case at least ten members of the public, gathered usually from passers-by in the street, take part, and thus it will be seen how unlikely it is that any deliberate unfairness would escape notice. Circumstances may arise under any system of safeguards in which a doubt is possible. The only way to meet these is to give at the trial a truthful and impartial account of the way in which the identification took place and let the Court judge of the reliability and value of the evidence.

'When a detective undertakes an investigation it is his business to ascertain the available evidence by all legitimate and common-sense means. There are many things he sees and hears which are not immediately relevant evidence, for a great part must necessarily be hearsay and inference. As far as possible he has to find witnesses who can give direct evidence on essential points. Hence the reason for such things as statements and identification parades. In the end, every bit of evidence has to be proved of some witness – even a document or a bloodstain has to be sworn to. Human nature being what it is, witnesses will sometimes make mistakes, or consciously or unconsciously distort the truth. No witness is infallible, although there is a tendency among some people to think that a certain type of scientific evidence cannot be doubted. In fact, experts are no more immune from mistakes than any other folk. I would much sooner accept the word of an intelligent and disinterested man in the street when he says at a particular time and place a definite event occurred than that of a gentleman who asserts opinions and theories as if they were unchallengeable facts.'

Given this, the question as to why Craswell did not attend an identification parade will regrettably remain unanswered. It will also always remain unknown why the jury took only twelve minutes to unanimously acquit Healy, but Wensley's view that the judge erred too much on the side of caution is strengthened when you consider Craswell's evidence. Could there have been any doubt about his identification of the prisoner given his obvious reluctance to get involved and claim that he would never recognise the man again? Could this man's evidence be so surely relied upon that a jury was prepared to send a man to the gallows? Defence counsel made much of the fact that Craswell was incapable of saying what type of hat the man in the shop was wearing, and surely he must have noticed such a simple matter. After all, Mavis Smith was able to recall that on the night in question Healy was wearing a brown suit and cap. But witnesses are not machines. They are going about their lives not realising that what they are seeing is to become important evidence at a trial. It is wholly realistic for a witness to remember what they saw and heard in part. But of course, it was not only Craswell's evidence that was put before the jury, and they were required to take everything into account when deciding their verdict.

The trial

The reasons why, after a prolonged investigation and dramatic trial, the jury were quick to unanimously acquit will never be known. It is the beauty of a democratic process that such matters remain secret. But it doesn't stop the questions and hypotheses. First and foremost, though, the fact remains that Healy was found not guilty and he is innocent. Nothing can change that. Nor should it. But in any interpretation of history it is right to pose questions and seek debate. The obvious conclusion is that the police got the wrong man. It wasn't Healy. But leaving that aside for a moment, to what extent did it play on the juror's mind that Reed declared this an accident? The lawyers didn't use this as a plank of their defence, nor was retired Superintendent Reed required to give evidence (though retired Sergeant Boarder did) to explain his rationale. It would have been an interesting cross-examination and one I feel sure that Judge Darling would have relished. Was it because he was clearly seen as a weakness to the prosecution case? But if that was so, why didn't the defence team summons him?

The injuries to Healy's finger were subject to much scrutiny. Did the injuries exist? The doctors thought so, but eleven out of the thirteen people who either knew or worked with Healy at Kryn and Lahy said they didn't see any wounds to his finger in the days after the murder. Neither, of course, did they see Healy fall over in the snow as he had claimed in his statement to the police. There was, however, one witness who was perfect for raising the question of whether Healy was sporting a bandaged finger in the days after the discovery of the body, yet there is nothing to suggest he was even asked; Percy Gigg. Healy said he went to the Plough and Dial at midday on the Monday. Gigg confirms that. He most certainly would be able to say whether or not his hand was bandaged. There is nothing in his statement about it and neither is he asked by any of the defence team. Odd.

If the injuries did exist, were they likely to have been caused by a dog bite? Again, the doctors thought so. It was a doubt that must have registered in the minds of the jurors. Surely, if the injuries were as bad as the police assumed they would be, they would have been seen. But it is likely that Craswell was seen as the pivotal point. None of the other witnesses had any reason to lie or exaggerate. As the trial judge stated, can there be any doubt about who is speaking the truth? Either Healy is lying or all the other witnesses are. But Craswell was different. He was the closest you will get to the witness seeing the murderer standing over the body with the smoking gun. And if it was wholly convinced as to his reliability, the jury knew it would be sending a man, a war hero, to the gallows. Once doubt was sown in minds over this point, there would have been grave difficulty in returning a guilty verdict.

The newspapers reported that outside the court there was 'unmistakable sympathy' shown towards the acquitted prisoner. I venture to suggest that these were fellow lodgers from the Irish community and servicemen, themselves affected by the horrors of war. It wasn't long after this that letters to editors of other newspapers revealed how many felt that any ex-serviceman charged with serious offences should only be tried by a jury of men who themselves had been witness to trench warfare. But there is something else which adds a little credibility to Healy's accusation that he and his wife were unpopular in Hitchin and this was all a ruse to oust them from the community. Irish labourers were a common sight in mainland Britain after the war, and clearly Annie Smith wasn't averse to having them as tenants and getting their rent money. But the Irish were generally viewed with some scepticism. Apart from the growing nationalist call of Irish independence about which many English people would have been ambivalent, a certain level of animosity remained over the issue of conscription, which had been introduced in January 1916. All men between the ages of eighteen and forty-one were conscripted into the army, where they would receive a salary of one shilling a week. Yet, Irishmen were exempt from this piece of emergency legislation and they filled the workforce void, which attracted a higher wage, while sons and husbands of the rest of Britain, as well as many Irishmen who did not wait to be conscripted but enlisted willingly, were slaughtered on the battlefields. Much hostility had been directed towards the Irish community as a whole and indeed many employers refused to hire them. Could it have been in the minds of the jurors that perhaps, just perhaps, there was an element of spite in the accusations? If you subscribe to that theory, then it was in the minds of all twelve jurors and all the prosecution witnesses were tainted with the same brush.

Case for the Crown

The prosecution case was a conglomerate of circumstantial evidence; it often is. Rarely is a jury presented with a series of people who witnessed the fatal blows. The murder took place, so said the Crown, shortly after 8.30pm on Saturday, 25 January; the victim was last seen alive around this time, passing neighbours saw the shop unusually still open after 9pm and thuds and moans were heard coming from within the shop. Shortly before this, Healy was seen hanging around outside the shop, acting furtively, by two people who lived in the same house as him only a few hundred yards away, and a few minutes later he was identified as someone in the shop buying tobacco and matches. He had been due back home at 9pm after a night at the pub, yet he didn't in fact return until 10.30pm, when, out of character, he disappeared upstairs to his room and wasn't seen again until the next morning. So, at the time of the murder he had no alibi and therefore opportunity. Prior to the murder he was broke, unable to pay his rent, but somehow, that week, he had acquired money, had settled his debts, bought new clothes (despite his denials), was coming home drunk in the evenings and even sent money to his sister in Ireland. Therefore, he had a motive. He lied about his being in Ridgley's shop in recent times and knew full well that she had money in her house. He wasn't afraid of animals; he had worked on farms in the past and his past army experience had probably made him indifferent to violence. The next day he was seen nursing a wounded finger on his right hand, injuries consistent with a dog bite. Bloodstained bedding and clothing, torn clothing, was found in his room. He owned khaki handkerchiefs. He was a pipe smoker; therefore, he used tobacco and matches. He was a man used to violence. He had a violent past and had been witness to the horrors of trench warfare, dismissing out of hand how Mrs Ridgley must have met a horrible death. The levels of violence used on the two victims, including the dragging of the dying woman by her hair, fitted with Healy's attitude to death. His indifference to, and his refusal to speak about the murder to his workmates or other lodgers in the house is not an evidential issue, although it would have played on the minds of the investigating officers.

Case for the Defence

The defence case was simple; everyone was either mistaken or lying. The only reason why witnesses told these lies was because Healy and his wife were unwelcome in Hitchin and there had been a conspiracy to oust them. Fabricating a murder charge against him was the way to achieve that. In support of this, there was evidence to show that he either couldn't have committed the murder or everything the prosecution had relied upon as evidence could be explained. Firstly, and this was the major point, if Ridgley was attacked in such a violent manner leaving blood all over the house, surely the murderer would have been covered from head to toe in stains. And surely, if the murderer had plundered the property in the way that the prosecution had made out, there would be fingerprints everywhere. There was nothing forensically to connect the defendant to the premises. Nothing. Even the handkerchief the police found in his possession when they searched him at the police station wasn't khaki. The witnesses who said they saw him inside or outside the shop were at best mistaken, at worst, liars, and it shouldn't be forgotten that the crucial witness, Craswell, saw two men in the shop, the other one never being identified. The injuries to Healy's hand happened at work, and indeed some witnesses were certain that in the days after the attack he bore no evidence of a wounded hand. He acknowledged he had no money before the murder was committed and that was why it would have been impossible for him to have been the man buying the tobacco and matches. Similarly, he had money after the murder as he had received his army gratuity payment that week. Not only was there grave doubt about the case, but quite simply, the police had got the wrong man.

This particular defence sparks an interesting debate. If true, then Healy was innocent; as indeed he remains to this day. But if not true, it was a risky line to adopt. On another day, another twelve men on a jury may not have given him the benefit of the doubt. But Healy had the opportunity to present himself as insane and therefore not liable to be convicted of murder. His mother was insane. He was, in modern parlance, psychotic and not in control of his violent behaviour. He had been exposed to the extremes of war, and in 1919 it was routine for sympathy to be given to returning soldiers. Healy was a product of the war. His partiality to violence was there before, but it was the adventures of war which drove him on. He had been taught the value of force as a temporary expedient for gaining one's end. It led to excesses which made him a danger to society. Many men had been affected in this way, and it was hardly surprising, since governments had created an orgy of lawlessness. It was a defence which would have been easily understood. But he didn't adopt the defence of insanity, perhaps because he feared being detained indefinitely under mental health rules or simply because he was neither mad nor guilty.

So, who killed Mrs Ridgley?

I said at the beginning of this chapter that it is unhelpful to examine a hundred-year-old murder through twenty-first century eyes, but in this final section I expose a fascinating element of this matter which appears to have gone unnoticed by Wensley, the Director of Public Prosecutions and Healy and his defence team. If it wasn't Healy who committed this murder, then who was it? I am going to return to the scene of the murder and the minutes leading up to those fatal blows and start by identifying some of those people who went into Mrs Ridgley's shop and became the focus of attention.

At some time after 8pm, eleven-year-old Arthur Massey went into the shop to buy some wood, and while in there he saw a man who was wearing a hard hat, a collar and tie, an overcoat and had pimples on his face. About the same time, Nellie Ludford came out of the shop and saw a man outside who was wearing a bowler hat though she couldn't say whether this man actually went inside. About the same time, William Craswell went into the shop and of course became a crucial witness. It cannot be said with absolute certainty that the man Massey and Ludford saw was Craswell, but given the timings it is a reasonable assumption. Photographs I have found in the archives show a picture of a man fitting this description, including the bowler hat, collar and tie and overcoat. This is highly likely to be Craswell. Why else would this man be photographed if it wasn't to be used in a newspaper article, and had Healy been found guilty, it is likely it would have been used. The quality of the photograph is such that pimples cannot be seen on his face, and it is indeed very unfortunate that there is no description of Craswell from the police, but everything points to this being a reasonable conclusion. In any event, Craswell of course admits to being the man in the shop, but it is *his* seemingly unprobed evidence that is intriguing. This is what he says in his very first statement on 7 February, when he presents himself to the police over a week before the name Healy drops into the police net:

'I went into her shop about twenty past eight on Saturday night the 25th January, 1919 to make a purchase and remained talking to her [Ridgley] about 5 or 10 minutes. She kept her matches and tobacco underneath the counter. When I left no one was in the shop. A man had been in to buy some matches or tobacco, he was a regular customer. I don't know his name [whom he later identified as Healy]. Just before I left and after the other man had gone out a man came into the passage not as far as the shop, and asked Mrs Ridgley for something she had not got and he then left. I think he asked for cigarettes but am not sure.'

Pause for a moment. When Craswell gave this statement to the police they had no idea who they were looking for and it was crucial to identify everyone in that shop as potential witnesses, hence the importance of Ludford and Mansell being found and interviewed. Therefore, the man who had bought the cigarettes was as important as the man who hadn't. Both were potential witnesses. A week later, attention switches to Healy because of all the reasons identified in this book, but this makes the man in the passageway, who didn't buy anything, no less important. He needed to be traced to find out what he saw. He may even have been able to corroborate Craswell in identifying Healy. Yet it appears he wasn't found. Given Healy's acquittal, does it not lend itself to this question? Was the man in the passageway the murderer? Why did Healy's defence team not say to the magistrates at the remand hearings or the barrister at the trial to the jury, 'Who was that other man in the shop? Can you be sure that he is not the real killer?' Why didn't Wensley use the newspapers to ask for this man to come forward? Was it because Healy had become so obviously the murderer that the other man had ceased being important? It is a gaping hole.

This uncomfortable aspect of the investigation gathers momentum when examining more papers I found that were stored away in a dusty archive seventy-five miles away in Hampshire. It had always been a mystery to me why papers and photographs, wholly unconnected to Hampshire, were filed away on the shelves of the Hampshire Constabulary History Society, although the discovery of these later papers may start to shed some light on that. One of the documents I found was a beautifully handwritten, eleven-page report by Alf Kirby. It is dated 19 June, the day *after* Healy's acquittal. I will discuss why I think this report was written in the first place shortly, but for now I will focus on two short sentences in the report which stand out as incongruous. The report is clearly outlining Kirby's involvement in the investigation, particularly his finding of the body, but suddenly, and out of context, he states:

'Enquiries were made by us and various statements taken, either in the street or in person's houses. A man named Worbey Dixon was seen by Inspectors Bowyer and Warren, and his house and premises examined.'

Now, I have no idea about who Dixon was and I am not seeking to attribute Ridgley's death to him in any way but his mention raises two issues. Firstly, if you critically analyse the Ridgley murder in the light of Healy's acquittal, would you not think that the unknown man who went into Ridgley's shop and Worbey Dixon could be one and the same? Which leads into the second point; why was Dixon spoken to by two inspectors at all? Take your mind back to 27 January when Bowyer and Warren were at the house making enquiries (and it would seem that this was the only day they were working together). We know that between them and Reed over the next couple of days they formed the opinion that death was due to accident. So why did they speak to Dixon and search his house? Surely, it could only have been that they knew they were dealing with a murder. They identified Dixon, somehow, as someone of interest, so much so that they searched his house. What were they looking for? Bloodstained items? Money? Anything which could have indicated that he was involved with Ridgley's death? Either way, it can be argued that it shows that in those early hours, and before Reed arrived, they were thinking murder. Everyone was saying the same; Kirby, Sutton and, arguably, Doctor Grellett.

Turning to the reasons why the report was written, I can only offer a view. Healy's acquittal was a surprise. Despite the good work carried out by Wensley, the case would have been one of embarrassment for Hertfordshire Constabulary, and now that the matter remained unsolved, questions needed to be asked. Two notable questions. To what extent was Reed liable for the acquittal, and if Ridgley was murdered and Healy wasn't the killer, who was? The starting point for such an enquiry is to review the evidence firstly around Reed's involvement and then the case as a whole. The papers and photographs found in Hampshire relate solely to Reed's involvement, and I think it is likely that the man most embarrassed about the acquittal was the fastidious, pedantic and proud chief constable, Alfred Letchworth Law. Having turned to Scotland Yard for a review of Reed's conclusion, he had been pleased that a man had been eventually charged with murder, but now he had been acquitted, he wasn't going to let the dust settle. He wanted it reviewed again. Only this time he turned to his old friend and colleague from his army days, and now Chief Constable of Hampshire County Constabulary, Major St Andrew Bruce Warde. However, since there is no evidence I can find that a further review was, in fact, ever carried out, it may be that my conclusion is incorrect. There must be a logical reason for the papers to be lodged in the Hampshire Constabulary archives but I fear this aspect will remain a mystery.

The question as to the identity of Ridgley's murderer seems to have faded into the mists of time until the 1930s when a reporter for the *Thomson's Weekly News*, Norman Hastings, wrote a long article, entitled, 'Innocent Man's Narrow Escape From Being Hanged'. He summarises the case, erroneously on occasions, and emphasises the dangers of convicting someone on the basis of circumstantial evidence. Many innocent people, he argued, had been convicted and this was yet another case where justice was almost evaded. All of the circumstantial evidence, the bloodstaining, the money, the dog bites, could be explained away and to acquit Healy was undoubtedly the correct verdict.

I am always reluctant to offer an opinion, for mine of course, carries no more weight than anyone else's. But I am often asked the question, so I should not shy away from offering my thoughts.

I have had the benefit of reading the original papers and as much contemporary information as I have been able to find, coupled with a sharpened insight into the methods of policing and court procedures at the time. It is no use arguing that had things been different, and the matter dealt with as a murder at the outset, there would probably have been a different outcome. Equally, it is necessary to dismiss any knowledge of Healy's violent behaviour in the years building up to 1919; quite rightly, it is not an indicator of guilt.

But, when the detail of all the circumstantial evidence is taken into account: the sudden possession of money; injuries consistent with a dog bite; bloodstaining on his clothes; him being seen inside and outside the shop just before the attack; his inability to alibi himself: his wife's contradiction of his timings and his basic defence that every witness was lying, I think it improbable that Healy was not the murderer. That is quite different, of course, from saying that he should have been convicted. I am minded to agree with Norman Hastings that, taking everything into account, Healy should have been given the benefit of the doubt.

And finally

In Wensley's memoirs, *Forty Years of Scotland Yard: A record of lifetime's Service in the Criminal Investigation Department*, the murder in Hitchin warrants only half a page of dialogue. This is not a criticism as it is one in which he genuinely felt he had failed and was at a disadvantage from the moment he was first called. Moreover, it was dwarfed by countless investigations in London. However, the tireless effort he and his colleagues placed into this investigation is worthy of wider exposure and demonstrates the extraordinary endeavour injected into a hitherto unknown tragedy. More importantly, the name of Elizabeth Ridgley, murdered on 25 January 1919, will no longer be just a vague memory on an unmarked grave.

Postscript

Having completed the writing of this book, new information came to light which adds a final twist to the story. Given the work carried out by Constable Alfred Kirby and him being congratulated by Wensley for his efforts, it is somewhat extraordinary that in August 1919 he was disciplined by the chief constable for his negligent handling of property found in Nightingale Road and Radcliffe Road. He was officially reprimanded and resigned on 3 September 1919, probably a very despondent man. Out of all the negligence displayed in this matter, he alone was singled out for disciplinary action.

I am very grateful to members of the Hertfordshire Constabulary Historical Society for uncovering this important aspect.

Select Bibliography

Books

ABRAHAMS, G., 1964. *Police Questioning and the Judges' Rules*. London: Oyez Publications

BROWN, D.G. and TULLETT,T., 1988. *Bernard Spilsbury: Famous Murder Cases of the Great Pathologist*. New York: Dorset Press

BROWNE, D.G., 1956. *The Rise of Scotland Yard*. London: George G. Harrap & Co. Ltd

BROWNE, D.G. and TULLETT, E.V., 1951. *Bernard Spilsbury: His Life and Cases*. London: George G. Harrap

CARLIN, F., (1927) *Reminiscences of an Ex-Detective*. London: Hutchinson & Co

CONNELL, R and STRATTON, S., 2003. *Hertfordshire Murders*. Stroud. History Press

EMSLEY, C., 2005. *Hard Men: Violence in England since 1750*. London: Hambledon and London

EMSLEY, C., 2009. *The Great British Bobby*. London: Quercus

FISHER, S., 1999. *Lust, Dust and Cobblestones*. Baldock: Sue Fisher

GAUTE, J.H.H. and ODELL, R., 1982. *Murder 'Whatdunnit'*. London: Harrap

KIRBY, D., 2014. *Whitechapel's Sherlock Holmes*. Barnsley: Pen and Sword

LAMBOURNE, G., 1984. *The Fingerprint Story*. London: Harrap Ltd

LAW, A., 1923. *Police Systems in Urban Districts*. London: S King & Son Ltd

LOGAN, G., 1935. *Wilful Murder*. London: Eldon Press

MARJORIBANKS, E., 1950. *Famous Trials of Marshall Hall*. Middlesex: Penguin

NEIL, A.F., 1932. *Forty Years of Man-hunting*. London: Jarrolds

OSBORN, N., 1969. *The Story of Hertfordshire Police*. Letchworth: Hertfordshire Countryside

PRINGLE, N. and TREVERSH, J., 1991. *150 Years Policing in Watford District and Hertfordshire County*. Luton: Radley Shaw Publishing

RHODES, H.T.F., 1933. *Clues and Crime*. London: John Murray

ROOME, H.D. and ROSS, R.E.. 1918. *Archbold's Criminal Pleading, Evidence and Procedure.* 25th Edition. London: Sweet and Maxwell

ROSE, A., 2007. *Lethal Witness.* Kent State University Press

SAVILL, S., 1913. *The Police Service of England and Wales.* London: John Kempster

SMITH, S., 1959. *Mostly Murder.* London: The Companion Book Club

TULLETT, T., 1979. *Strictly Murder.* London: Bodley Head

WARD, J., 1998. *Crime Busting: Breakthroughs in Forensic Science.* London: Blandford Press

WENSLEY, F.P., 1931. *Forty Years of Scotland Yard: A record of lifetime's service in the Criminal Investigation Department.* New York: Garden City Publishing Company

Newspapers

Daily Chronicle

Daily Mail

Daily Sketch

Evening News

Evening Standard

Hertfordshire Express

Hertfordshire Mercury

Irish Times

The Kerryman

Leicester Mercury

News of the World

Salisbury Times and South Wilts Gazette

Thomson's Weekly News

The Times

Times: History of the War 1914 Illustrated

Websites

http://www.hertspastpolicing.org.uk/

Other records

British Army medal index cards 1914–1920. The National Archives reference WO/372/9

Hertfordshire Constabulary records

Kelly's Directory, England

Police Review and Parade Gossip

Royal Army Medical Corps Training 1911 (reprinted 1914)

The National Archives crime files; references MEPO 3/260, MEPO 3/262B, DPP 1/61

Thom's Directory, Ireland

War Diary of 13 Field Ambulance (5th Division) National Archives Reference WO 95/1540/1

Wensley Family Archives, Bishopsgate Institute, London

Notes

Chapter 1

1. Statements of Mary and George Rutland, 24 February 1919, The National Archives reference MEPO 3/260.
2. Statement of Police Constable Alfred Kirby, 22 February 1919, The National Archives reference MEPO 3/260.
3. Statement of Gertrude Day, 21 February 1919, The National Archives reference MEPO 3/260.
4. Report of PC 109 Kirby, 29 January 1919, The National Archives reference MEPO 3/260.
5. Statement of Frank Arthur Wheeler, 7 February 1919, The National Archives reference MEPO 3/260.
6. Statement of Edwin Sutton, 10 February 1919, The National Archives reference MEPO 3/260.

Chapter 3

7. Statement of Police Constable Alfred Kirby, 8 February 1919, The National Archives reference MEPO 3/260.
8. Report of DCI Wensley, 15 February 1919, The National Archives reference MEPO 3/260.

Chapter 5

9. Statement of Walter Bowyer, 14 February 1919, The National Archives reference MEPO 3/260.
10. Statement of Annie Withey, undated, The National Archives reference MEPO 3/260.
11. Statement of Inspector Frederick William Warren, 10 February 1919, The National Archives reference MEPO 3/260.
12. Statement of Louisa Roach, 27 January 1919, The National Archives reference MEPO 3/260.

13. Statement of Frank Wheeler, undated, The National Archives reference MEPO 3/260.
14. Statement of Inspector Frederick William Warren, 10 February 1919, The National Archives reference MEPO 3/260.
15. Statements of Walter Bowyer and Frederick William Warren, The National Archives reference MEPO 3/260.
16. Statement of William Pennington Grellett, undated, The National Archives reference MEPO 3/260.

Chapter 6

17. Statement of Thomas Dillon, undated and handwritten, The National Archives reference MEPO 3/260.
18. Statement of Michael Healy, undated and handwritten, The National Archives reference MEPO 3/260 and 1901 census return.
19. Statements of Constable Michael Lillis, undated and handwritten and Michael Healy, undated and handwritten, The National Archives reference MEPO 3/260.
20. Statement of John McKenna, undated and handwritten, The National Archives reference MEPO 3/260.
21. Statements of Michael Healy, undated and handwritten and Dr Timothy Buckley, undated and handwritten, The National Archives reference MEPO 3/260.
22. Statement of Constable Michael Lillis, undated and handwritten, The National Archives reference MEPO 3/260.
23. Statement of John Moon, handwritten, The National Archives reference MEPO 3/260.

Chapter 7

24. Report of Superintendent Reed, 29 January 1919, The National Archives reference MEPO 3/260.
25. Statement of Police Constable Alfred Kirby, 22 February 1919, The National Archives reference MEPO 3/260.
26. Statement of Inspector Frederick William Warren, 10 February 1919, The National Archives reference MEPO 3/260.
27. Report of Superintendent Reed, 29 January 1919, The National Archives reference MEPO 3/260.
28. Report of DCI Wensley, 15 February 1919, p.21, The National Archives reference MEPO 3/260.

Chapter 8

29. Statement of Catherine Lawrence, 19 February 1919, The National Archives reference MEPO 3/260.

Chapter 9

30. Statement of Mary Chandler, 6 February 1919, The National Archives reference MEPO 3/260.
31. Statement of Alfred Kirby, 20 February 1919, The National Archives reference MEPO 3/260.
32. Report of Superintendent Reed, 2 February 1919, The National Archives reference MEPO 3/260.
33. Report of Superintendent Reed, 29 January 1919, The National Archives reference MEPO 3/260.
34. Statement of William Goldsmith, 13 February 1919, The National Archives reference MEPO 3/260.
35. Report of DCI Wensley, 15 February 1919, The National Archives reference MEPO 3/260.
36. Extract from shop account books produced by William Waters, The National Archives reference MEPO 3/260 p.176.
37. Report of Superintendent Reed, 29 January 1919, The National Archives reference MEPO 3/260.
38. Report of Superintendent Reed, 29 January 1919, The National Archives reference MEPO 3/260.

Chapter 10

39. Report of Superintendent Reed, 2 February 1919, The National Archives reference MEPO 3/260.
40. Report of Superintendent Reed, 2 February 1919, The National Archives reference MEPO 3/260.

Chapter 13

41. Report of DCI Wensley, 15 February 1919, The National Archives reference MEPO 3/260.
42. Statement of Mary Chandler, 6 February 1919, The National Archives reference MEPO 3/260.
43. Report of DCI Wensley, 15 February 1919, The National Archives reference MEPO 3/260.
44. Statements of PC William Waters, 12 February 1919 and DS William McBride, 13 February 1919.

45. Statement of Inspector Frederick William Warren, 10 February 1919, The National Archives reference MEPO 3/260.
46. Statement of Annie Withey, 7 February 1919, The National Archives reference MEPO 3/260.
47. Statement of Frank Arthur Wheeler, 7 February 1919, The National Archives reference MEPO 3/260.
48. Statements of Louisa Roach and Leslie Roach, 7 February 1919, The National Archives reference MEPO 3/260.

Chapter 14

49. Statement of Emma Gravestock, 14 February 1919, The National Archives reference MEPO 3/260.
50. Statement of Arthur Massey, 12 February, The National Archives reference MEPO 3/260.
51. Statement of William Augustus Craswell, 7 February 1919, The National Archives reference MEPO 3/260.
52. Statement of Kate Gilbert, 11 February 1919, The National Archives reference MEPO 3/260.
53. Report of DCI Wensley, 2 February 1919 and statement of John Chandler, 12 February 1919, The National Archives reference MEPO 3/260.

Chapter 15

54. Coroner's Warrant, 13 February 1919, The National Archives reference MEPO 3/260.
55. Statement of Bernard H. Spilsbury, 24 February 1919, The National Archives reference MEPO 3/260.

Chapter 16

56. The existence of this letter is only referred to once in a post-trial report by Alfred Kirby. The letter hasn't been found nor are its exact contents known, although they can calculated with more or less certainty based on Wensley's report, 15 February 1919, p.29, and letter written by Annie Healy, 18 February 1919.
57. Report of Alfred Kirby, 19 June 1919, The National Archives reference MEPO 3/260.
58. Statement of Frederick Wensley, 20 February 1919, The National Archives reference MEPO 3/260.
59. Report of Alfred Kirby, 19 June 1919, The National Archives reference MEPO 3/260.

60. Statement of John Healy, 15 February 1919, The National Archives reference MEPO 3/260

61. Statement of Annie Healy, 15 February 1919, The National Archives reference MEPO 3/260.

62. Statement of Alfred Kirby, 20 February 1919, and statements of William Waters, one undated and the other 20 February 1919, The National Archives reference MEPO 3/260.

63. Statement of Annie Smith, 24 May 1919, The National Archives reference MEPO 3/260.

64. Statements of Annie and Mavis Smith, 15 February 1919, The National Archives reference MEPO 3/260.

65. Statement of Bernard Smith, 20 February 1919, The National Archives reference MEPO 3/260.

66. Statement of DCI Wensley, 20 February 1919, The National Archives reference MEPO 3/260.

67. Statement of William Pennington Grellett, 21 February 1919, The National Archives reference MEPO 3/260.

68. Report of DCI Wensley, 15 February 1919, The National Archives reference MEPO 3/260.

Chapter 17

69. Statements of Louisa Powis and Florence Dickinson, 21 February 1919, The National Archives reference MEPO 3/260.

70. Statement of Albert William Jenkins, 27 January 1919, The National Archives reference MEPO 3/260. However, the date of this statement cannot be correct and is a typing error. It is likely to have been taken on 27 February.

71. Statement of William McBride, 24 February 1919, The National Archives reference MEPO 3/260.

72. Statement of Louisa Hawkins, undated, The National Archives reference MEPO 3/260.

73. Statements of Percy Wallace Gigg, 20 and 24 February 1919, The National Archives reference MEPO 3/260.

Chapter 18

74. Statement of Annie Healy, 20 February 1919, The National Archives reference MEPO 3/260.

75. Statement of Annie Healy, 20 February 1919, The National Archives reference MEPO 3/260.

76. Statement of Mavis Barbara Smith, 24 May 1919, The National Archives reference MEPO 3/260.

Chapter 19

77. Statement of Annie Smith, 24 May 1919, The National Archives reference MEPO 3/260.

78. Statement of Lancelot Babbage Alcombe, 27 February 1919, The National Archives reference MEPO 3/260.

79. The National Archives reference MEPO 3/260.

80. Statement of Ernest Jeavons, 24 February 1919, The National Archives reference MEPO 3/260.

81. Statements of Thomas Henry Cain, Arthur Smyth, Daniel Boyle, Richard James Reeves, 24 February 1919 and Harry Foster, William Spensley and William Henry Lane, 25 February 1919, The National Archives reference MEPO 3/260.

82. Statements of Frederick Barker, 25 February 1919 and Frederick Hewitt, 26 February 1919, The National Archives reference MEPO 3/260.

83. Statements of Richard James Reeves, Frederick Barker, Frederick Hewitt, ibid and Arthur Cooper, 25 February 1919, The National Archives reference MEPO 3/260.

84. Statements of Daniel Boyle and Arthur Cooper, ibid.

85. Entry on Hatfield registry file addressed to the commissioner, dated 26 February 1919, The National Archives reference MEPO 3/260.

86. Statement of Nellie Ludford, 25 February 1919, The National Archives reference MEPO 3/260.

Chapter 20

87. Report of DCI Wensley, 24 March 1919, The National Archives reference MEPO 3/260.

88. Report of DCI Wensley, 24 March 1919, The National Archives reference MEPO 3/260.

89. Report of DCI Wensley, 24 March 1919, The National Archives reference MEPO 3/260.

90. Statement of William Augustus Craswell, 23 May 1919, The National Archives reference MEPO 3/260.

91. Statements of William Augustus Craswell, 3 March 1919, 16 May 1919 and 23 May 1919, The National Archives reference MEPO 3/260.

Chapter 21

92. Statement of John Moon, handwritten, The National Archives reference MEPO 3/260.

93. Registered postal packet, National Archives reference MEPO 3/260.
94. Statements of Bridget Cooney and Hannah Healy, 3 March 1919, and Margaret Healy, undated, The National Archives reference MEPO 3/260. It is interesting that Annie Healy was capable of writing letters yet signed her witness statement at the police station indicating that she was illiterate.

Chapter 22

95. Report of DCI Wensley, 24 March 1919, The National Archives reference MEPO 3/260.
96. Statement of Ellen Rosina Rowe, 6 March 1919, The National Archives reference MEPO 3/260.
97. Statement of Annie Smith, 8 March 1919, The National Archives reference MEPO 3/260.

Chapter 23

98. Statement of Harry Charles Taylor, 12 March 1919, The National Archives reference MEPO 3/260.

Chapter 24

99. Report of DCI Wensley, 24 March1919, The National Archives reference MEPO 3/260.
100. Letter from Chief Constable Law to commissioner of police, 24 March 1919, The National Archives reference MEPO 3/260.
101. Report of DCI Wensley, 24 March 1919, The National Archives reference MEPO 3/260.

Chapter 25

102. The sworn jurors were Thomas Adams, Henry Southwood Bailey, William Baker, George Ernest Brown, Francis Archibald Collier, Alfred Charles Darlington, Augustus Nelson Frisby, Ernest Basil Judd, Arthur Ewan McEwan, John Chappel Pigg, John Hugh Rolfe and Ernest Rose. South Eastern Circuit court records 1916–1919, The National Archives.
103. The witnesses called were Detective Constable Walters, Detective Sergeant McBride, Mary Chandler, George Rutland, Louisa and Leslie Roach, Gertrude Day, Police Constable Kirby, Superintendent Warren (previously inspector), William Goldsmith, Dr William Grellett, Bernard Smith, William Craswell, Annie Smith and Jens Christan Christiansen.

Chapter 26

104. *Hertfordshire Express*, 21 June 1919 and report of DCI Wensley, 23 June 1919, The National Archives reference MEPO 3/260.

105. Report of DCI Wensley, 23 June 1919, The National Archives reference MEPO 3/260. This final sentence about a case not being proven is not cited in any newspaper report.

Chapter 27

106. Letter dated 20 June 1919, The National Archives reference MEPO 3/260. Mathews died in January 1920, aged 70 years.

107. Report of DCI Wensley, 23 June 1919, The National Archives reference MEPO 3/260

108. Report of DCI Wensley, 24 March 1919, The National Archives reference MEPO 3/260.

109. The National Archives reference MEPO 3/260.

Chapter 28

110. Death record, registration number 1843339, Listowel.

Chapter 29

111. Report of DCI Wensley, 15 February 1919, The National Archives reference MEPO 3/260.

112. Report of DCI Wensley, 15 February 1919, p.21, The National Archives reference MEPO 3/260.

113. Wensley, F. P., 1931. *Forty Years of Scotland Yard: A record of lifetime's service in the Criminal Investigation Department.* New York: Garden City Publishing Company.

114. Report of Alfred Kirby, 19 June 1919, The National Archives reference MEPO 3/260.

Index

A HIDDEN STORY FOR ALMOST A HUNDRED YEARS, POLICE
INCOMPETENCE IS BROUGHT TO THE SURFACE.

POST-WAR POLICING LAID BARE.

WHEN ANGLO-IRISH TENSION WAS AT ITS HEIGHT, AN IRISH WAR
VETERAN WAS ACCUSED OF MURDER IN MAINLAND BRITAIN.

A CENTURY LATER, A NEW SUSPECT EMERGES.

IN 1919, when a shopkeeper and her dog were found dead in Hitchin, Hertfordshire
with brutal head injuries, there followed an extraordinary catalogue of events and a
local police investigation which concluded that both had died as a result of a tragic
accident. A second investigation by Scotland Yard led to the arrest of an Irish war
veteran, but the outcome was far from conclusive.

Written from the perspective of the main characters involved and drawing on
original and newly-discovered material, this book exposes the frailties of county
policing just after the First World War and how it led to fundamental changes in
methods of murder investigations.

Offering a unique balance of story-telling and analysis, the book raises a number
of unanswered questions. These are dealt with in the final chapter by the author's
commentary drawing upon his expertise.

Paul Stickler joined Hampshire Constabulary in 1978 and spent the majority
of his time in CID. He spent many years involved in murder investigations and
was seconded to the FBI Academy in Quantico, Virginia to study international
perspectives of crime investigation. Since his retirement in 2008 he has combined his
professional knowledge with his passion for history, researching murders in the first
half of the twentieth century. He spends his days delivering lectures to a wide range
of audiences. More can be found out about him on his website:
www.historicalmurders.com

UK **£14.99**
US **$29.95**

Cover design: Jon Wilkinson

ISBN 1526733854

9 781526 733856
www.**pen-and-sword**.co.uk

SCAN THE
QR CODE FOR
MORE
TITLES FROM
PEN & SWORD